KS3 POETRY PLUS

EMC KS3 Curriculum plus

KS3 POETRY PLUS

Written by Kate Oliver, Barbara Bleiman, Lucy Hinchliffe, Andrew McCallum and Lucy Webster

Edited by Barbara Bleiman and Andrew McCallum

Cover and chapter titles: Rebecca Scambler, www.rebeccascambler.com

English and Media Centre, 18 Compton Terrace, London, N1 2UN

© English and Media Centre, 2018

ISBN: 978-1-906101-59-6

Printed by: Stephens and George

Thanks to the staff and students at St Michael's, High Wycombe, in particular teachers Richard Long and Emily Hansbury and student Naomi-Lee.

With thanks to the following publishers, agents and picture libraries for permission to reproduce copyright material:

Miss Charlotte Brown by Felix Jung, Creative Commons license. Politicians from Plum written by Hollie McNish, published by Picador Poetry © Hollie McNish. Carcanet Press for Edwin Morgan – The Lochness Monster's Song; Sophie Hannah – Trainers All Turn Grey; Animals by Frank O'Hara, Carcanet. Sonnet (inspired by Sonnet 22) by Wendy Cope, by kind permission of United Agents. Permission for the use of three (3) lines from THE EARLIEST ENGLISH POEMS, translated by Michael Alexander (Penguin Classics 1966, 3rd edition 1991) Copyright © Michael Alexander, 1966, 1977, 1991. Inua Ellams for Dear Tina, Summit of flight, Ghetto van Gogh, Directions and video performances, with kind permission. Still I Rise by Maya Angelou from The Complete and Collected Poems, Virago 1994, reproduced by permission of Little Brown Group. Maryam Hussein: The Weight from Beautiful Like a Traffic Light, by kind permission of the Arvon Foundation and Lillian Baylis Technology School. Julius Chingono: As I Go, by permission of Irene Staunton (Weaver Books) on behalf of the author. Langston Hughes: Harlem (2) from THE COLLECTED POEMS OF LANGSTON HUGHES, published by Alfred A Knopf Inc, by permission of David Higham Literary, Film and TV agents. Inuit poem – v2, published in Nature and Identity in Cross-Cultural Perspective - GeoJournal Library 48 A. Buttimer (editor), L. Wallin (editor) p. 196-197 Publisher: Springer. I got 99 problems (video performance), by kind permission of Harry Baker. FAM (video performance) by Caleb Oluwafemi, by kind permission of Harry Baker. Peters Fraser & Dunlop Ltd for 'Only One of Me' by James Y Berry. Time Does Not Bring Relief by Edna St Vincent Millay Copyright 1931, © 1958 by Edna St. Vincent Millay and Norma Millay Ellis. Reprinted with permission of Elizabeth Barnett and Holly Peppe, Literary Executors, The Millay Society. City Lights Publishing and the Estate of Frank O'Hara for Lara Turner Has Collapsed by Frank O'Hara from Lunch Poems (City Lights, 1964). Hijab Scene No. 7, in E-mails from Scheherazad, by Mohja Kahf, Gainesville: University Press of Florida, 2003, pp.39. Reprinted with permission of the University Press of Florida. Robert Frost: Acquainted with the Night, The Road not taken, Nothing Gold Can Stay, Dust of Snow, by permission of Penguin Random House UK; Kate Wakeling and the Emma Press for The Instruction from Moon Juice, © Kate Wakeling and the Emma Press. Brian Bilston for Refugees and Love in the Time of Cauliflower. Faber and Faber Ltd for Maighdean Mara from Wintering Out by Seamus Heaney. 'Directions' from The Art of Drowning by Billy Collins, © 1995 Reprinted by permission of the University of Pittsburgh Press; 'the parents anniversary' by Lucy Thynne the winning entry to Foyle Young Poet of the Year Award 2017 was first published by The Poetry Society Run (poetrysociety.org.uk/competitions/foyle-young-poets-of-the-year-award/).

Every effort has been made to trace and acknowledge copyright, but if accidental infringement has been made, we would welcome information to redress the situation.

CONTENTS

Foreword for Teachers	4
Using KS3 Poetry Plus	5
Introduction for Pupils	6
Ten Things to do with a Poetry Anthology	7
What Is a Poem?	31
Say It Out Loud!	43
The Choices Poets Make	59
Lost in Translation	79
Study of a Poet: Robert Frost	91
Poets Speaking Out	107
Poems on the Theme of Love	125
Study of a Poet: Inua Ellams	145
KS3 Poetry Plus Anthology	169
Appendix	221

© ENGLISH & MEDIA CENTRE, 2018

KS3 POETRY PLUS
Foreword For Teachers

When poets and critics try to say what poetry is, they search for words to express its difference from other literary forms and other kinds of writing, the qualities that make it special. They use phrases like 'language made strange' or 'musical thought' or 'thoughts that breathe, and words that burn.' In teaching poetry to young people, it is important that this specialness is both experienced and understood by them – not just to help them to think about poetry in the ways that will ultimately support them in writing about poetry in exams but also to allow them to experience poetry in rich, rewarding and authentic ways. Poems are not like prose, nor are they written by poets in order to 'exemplify' poetic devices, such as alliteration, onomatopoeia, or enjambment. Poems are complex, they revel in multiple meanings and plays on words, on their connotations and associations, on playing with poetic conventions and creating subtle patterning of ideas, sounds and visual layout.

This book is written with these ideas in mind. The aim is to allow students to experience poems, enjoy them, learn more about how they work, discover the range of choices that poets make and develop the conceptual understandings (and associated literary vocabulary) to be able to think, talk and write about poetry in sensitive, sensible, honest and illuminating ways. Literary terms and concepts are taught along the way and students are encouraged to be selective and make judgements about what is of most interest in the poems they are encountering.

The book includes many opportunities for students to write poetry themselves. Sometimes, this is in order to understand more about how poems work and it might involve just a brief experiment, such as writing a few lines before or during an activity on a poem. Trying something out for yourself, making tiny little word changes, or writing before reading a poem can give valuable insight into the choices a poet has made. Sometimes, the writing of poems is for its own sake, though. Writing poetry has, historically, had an important place in the English curriculum, for good reason. It offers opportunities for self-expression. It provides a context for developing language in a condensed, intense, language-rich form in which every word and every grammatical choice counts. It provides scope for drafting, re-drafting, discussion of choices, performing and sharing. It gives students a taste of writing in a form that is becoming increasingly popular among young adults and gives them an entry into a literary world beyond the classroom.

While the nine units are each designed to be studied as a chunk, for instance over a few weeks, across Years 7-9, the ten activities that open the book are rather different. They offer scope for an individual lesson or two, from time to time, sprinkled throughout the Key Stage, to allow students to range across a collection of poems in more open-ended ways. This is a different kind of experience of poetry – freer, more exploratory, with reading for pleasure and thinking for yourself at the heart of the lessons. Organising the curriculum in chunks has many practical advantages but it means that students' encounters with poetry involve long gaps between each one. The 10 activities mitigate this and offer opportunities to refresh students' memories, revisit literary concepts and keep the poetry pot on the boil, while other work is being done.

Finally, we have looked for fresh angles, interesting poems that aren't necessarily the staples of published poetry resources, and ways of approaching poems that will teach particular aspects and ideas, rather than just 'here's another poem, here's another activity'. We hope that this will bring an exciting and invigorating new set of approaches that will lead to students feeling not only well-informed about poetry but also confident and enthusiastic about reading and writing about it.

Barbara Bleiman

USING KS3 POETRY PLUS

Using KS3 Poetry Plus

Accessing the Additional Resources

Additional resources are provided online to accompany *KS3 Poetry Plus*.

Downloadable worksheets

Download these from the 'Poetry Plus' page on the EMC website, under 'Additional Resources'. Search 'KS3 Poetry Plus' at https://www.englishandmedia.co.uk/ or go to https://www.englishandmedia.co.uk/publications/ks3-poetry-plus-print

Video clips

These are accessible from the video clips menu on the EMC home page or via the URLs below.

- **10 Things to Do with a Poetry Anthology**:
  https://www.englishandmedia.co.uk/video-clips/ks3-poetry-plus-sharing-a-poem

- **Say It Out Loud**:
  https://www.englishandmedia.co.uk/video-clips/ks3-poetry-plus-say-it-out-loud

- **Study of a Poet – Inua Ellams**:
  https://www.englishandmedia.co.uk/video-clips/ks3-poetry-plus-inua-ellams

The video clips are streamed from EMC's Vimeo site and cannot be downloaded. Please ensure your school security settings allow access to Vimeo before attempting to show these in the classroom.

You do not need to have registered an account on the EMC website to access these resources. Pupils can also access the clips outside of the classroom, in the library or at home.

Photocopiable pages

This publication is not photocopiable. However, page 93 ('Acquainted With the Night') can be copied.

Answers – and a warning!

Answers: The Appendix (pages 221-223) includes the answers for 'What is a Poem' (page 32), 'Author Study – Applying What You Know' and the three stanzas from James Berry's 'Haiku Moments 1' used in the activity on page 62. The full poem is in the Anthology on page 198. Frank O'Hara's 'Poem' referred to in the activity on pages 64-65 is in the Anthology on page 197. The poem for 'Choosing Line Breaks and Layout' on page 72 is in the Anthology on page 194.

A warning: The activity 'The Second Poem' on page 139 asks the teacher to talk about their own response to one of two poems selected by the class for further critical study. It might be worth taking the class vote at the end of a lesson to give you time to prepare this before the next lesson.

The Anthology

The poems in the Anthology on pages 169-220 are arranged broadly chronologically.

© ENGLISH & MEDIA CENTRE, 2018

KS3 POETRY PLUS
Introduction For Pupils

> 'I want to read more and learn more about it… I find it confusing because I don't know why people write poems… I don't know why it matters but I want to learn about why it matters to people who read it.'
>
> 'I think poems are special because they have something that stories don't have.'
>
> 'Whenever I'm alone I think of a poem in my head.'
>
> 'I think poetry is important and I really enjoy it.'
>
> 'In my opinion poetry doesn't matter. Don't get me wrong, it is interesting, but it doesn't matter.'

These are some things that some new Year 7 students said about poetry before they started studying it. Do you recognise any of the things they say as expressing your feelings and your view of poetry?

This book is all about discovering:

- What poetry is
- What makes it different from stories and other kinds of writing
- How it works
- What's enjoyable about it
- Why it matters, to other people, and to you.

It's also about introducing you to a wide range of poems from different times and places, by different kinds of writers, so that by the end of KS3 you will go away knowing some poems really well, and hopefully carrying some of them around with you, as favourites, for the rest of your life.

If you started KS3 loving poetry, we hope the activities will continue your journey of discovery, allowing you to choose poems you like and work on them, explore new ones and find out more about traditions of poetry. If you started KS3 less confident or a bit unsure about poetry, the activities will build up your confidence and understanding, to help you enjoy becoming more expert and knowledgeable about it.

Everything in this book is designed to get you thinking, encouraging you to explore your ideas and dig deeper into the craft of the writers. It will build up your knowledge and experience gradually and prepare you for poetry at GCSE.

And you'll also have the chance to do lots of poetry writing along the way – everything from little experiments and imitations to help you understand more about a poem, to drafting and crafting your own poems.

POETRY
ANTHOLOGY
TEN THINGS TO DO WITH A POETRY ANTHOLOGY

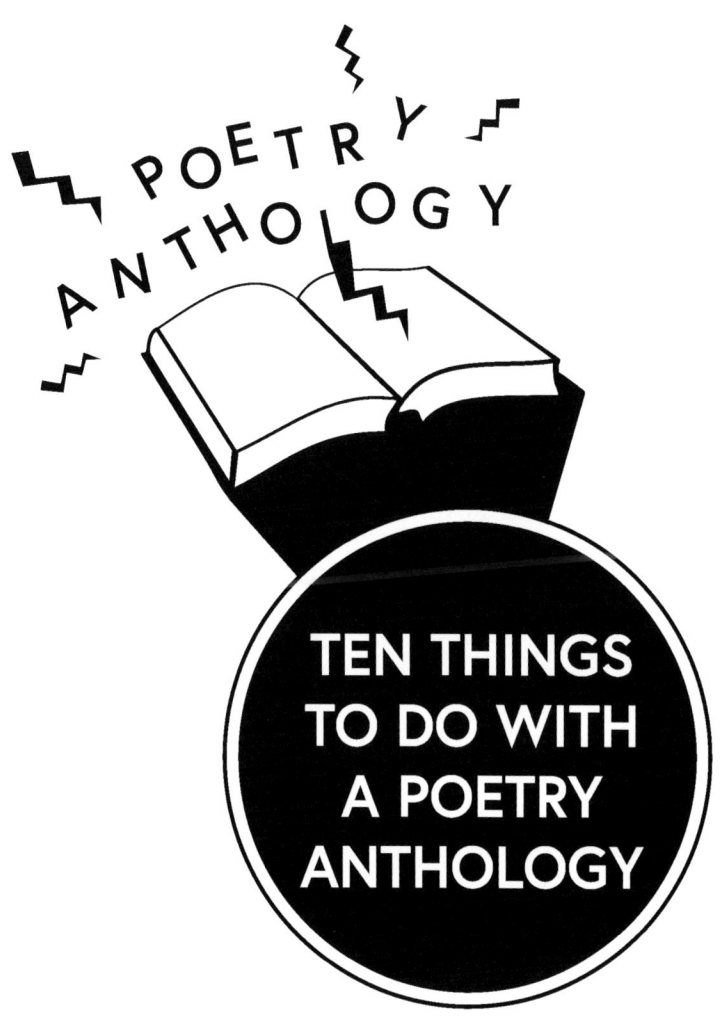

KS3 POETRY PLUS

1. Share With Your Class

Your teacher may start this lesson by reading to you a short poem they particularly like, then telling you a bit about what is special for them about the poem and their thoughts and feelings about it.

Stage 1

Choose a poem of your own

- On your own look through the poems in the Anthology section at the back of this book (see pages 169-220).

- Find one that you specially like. Take your time to choose. Don't be put off if you don't understand everything about it.

Think about:

- What you like about it – what made you choose it
- What interests or puzzles you
- What you think is special about it
- Any questions you have about it that you want to ask of other members of your group.

- Jot down a few notes on these things.

10 THINGS TO DO WITH AN ANTHOLOGY

Stage 2

Share your chosen poems in a group of three and prepare to introduce one poem to the whole class

- Read your poems aloud to each other.

- Talk about the poems and share why you chose them, anything that interests or puzzles you and any questions you want to ask each other.

- Compare the poems, for example 'Mine's like this… yours is like that.'

- Pick one poem that you all agree that you like.

- Prepare to read your chosen poem out loud to the whole class and present the reasons for your choice. Share out bits of the presentation between you.

Stage 3

Group presentations of a poem to the whole class

- Do your presentation and listen to those of other members of the class.

Stage 4

Exploratory writing (either in class, or for homework)

- Individually, write about your own first choice of poem, your group's choice or another poem you heard about in the presentations. The writing is for you, to get your ideas down and to sort out what you think. You could write about what you like, what interests you, what puzzles you, what's special about it, what thoughts you have about bits of the poem that are difficult or confusing. Use anything you've heard in the discussion in class but put down fresh ideas too.

This is not for assessment. On page 10 are the kinds of things you might find yourself saying, not as a checklist but as some prompts for your thinking. You might find yourself writing a lot on just one or two of them, or ignore them altogether because you have something else that has really struck you that you want to explore on paper.

© **ENGLISH & MEDIA CENTRE, 2018**

KS3 POETRY PLUS

Exploring a poem

- When I first read this poem I thought… because… Now I… because…
- I like the way it… The best example of this is…
- I noticed… I think the poet chose to do this in order to…
- At the beginning of the poem…
- By the end of the poem…
- I discovered that…
- The tone of the poem seems to be…
- I think the poem was written for/to… because…
- I would recommend this poem to… because…
- I think the most important idea in the poem is… I think this because…
- When the poet says… this makes me feel/think…
- I'm still puzzled by…
- I'm interested in the way…
- I think what this poet is trying to do is…
- I changed my mind about… because…
- The word/phrase/line '…' suggests… and makes me…
- My favourite bit is… because…
- Some people might think… I think…
- My overall feeling about the poem is…

10 THINGS TO DO WITH AN ANTHOLOGY

2. Write a Poem Diary – Living With a Poem

Getting to know a poem can take time. Sometimes, it's only when you've read it several times and become really familiar with it that your ideas start to take shape.

- Choose one poem from the Anthology (pages 169-220) that you'd like to spend a bit of time on. It doesn't have to be one that you find particularly easy or straightforward. It might be one that has interesting or confusing aspects.

- Read the poem you've chosen to yourself and then once out loud, then write some thoughts about it. What you write is for you only. It's like a diary, in which your record your genuine, honest ideas and feelings. For example, writing about the poem 'On Monsieur's Departure' (page 172):

> I was grabbed straight away by it being written by Queen Elizabeth I. We're doing that period in History. I didn't know she wrote poems. Did all kings and queens do that in those times? I wonder what 'prate' means? (Note to myself: ask or look it up.) I like the way it starts 'I grieve'. She's sad. But why doesn't she dare show she's unhappy. She's the queen isn't she? Why does she have to hide her love, if that's what she's doing? I like the way each of the first lines at the beginning starts 'I grieve…I love…I do…I seem.'

- Next lesson come back to the poem. Read it again. Perhaps read your poem diary again too – or don't, if you want to think completely afresh. Add to your writing about the poem.

- Next lesson, or next week, come back and read it again and add to your poem diary.

- Next lesson, or next week, see if you can learn any of your poem off by heart. When you've done this, go back to write in your diary anything about that experience. Did it make you notice anything new about the poem?

- At the end of the period of keeping the diary, read everything you've said about the poem. Write a final set of comments about what's changed for you since the beginning of the diary.

- Now try writing about the poem in a more structured way, this time for an outside audience – your teacher, or other people in your class. Pull together your thoughts, so you can explain your ideas about the poem in a clear, coherent way.

- Share your piece of writing with your teacher and/or other people in your class.

© ENGLISH & MEDIA CENTRE, 2018

KS3 POETRY PLUS

3. Classify a Poem – What Kind of 'Creature' Is It?

Poems can be described in different ways. They can fall into different types (for instance poems that tell a story, or short personal ones about a single thought or feeling). They might come from different traditions (for instance oral or written) or have different aspects that jump out at you as being especially important. In other words they can be 'classified' in different ways, almost as if they were a creature that can be described by its species and its most significant features.

Classifying an animal – what kind of animal is the stump-tailed macaque?

1. A stump-tailed macaque is a generalist mammal
2. Of the mammals, it's a primate
3. Of the primates, it's a simian
4. Of the simians, it's a non-hominoid simian
5. Of the non-hominoid simians, it's a catarrhine monkey (or Old World monkey)
6. Of the catarrhine monkeys, it's a cercopithecinae
7. Of the cercopithecinae, it's part of the papionini tribe
8. Of the papionini tribe, its genus is macaca, or macaque.
9. It's a stump-tailed macaque.

10 THINGS TO DO WITH AN ANTHOLOGY

Here is an example of how someone studying *literature*, rather than animals, might classify a poem. Unlike animals, you can't narrow down the classification quite so clearly. But nevertheless, you can move from big things to smaller things, depending on what seems important.

▪ Read Wendy Cope's poem 'Sonnet', written in response to Shakespeare's 'Sonnet 22'.

> **Sonnet by Wendy Cope**
>
> My glass can't quite persuade me I am old –
> In that respect my ageing eyes are kind –
> But when I see a photograph, I'm told
> The dismal truth: I've left my youth behind.
> And when I try to get up from a chair
> My knees remind me they are past their best.
> The burden they have carried everywhere
> Is heavier now. No wonder they protest.
> Arthritic fingers, problematic neck,
> Sometimes causing mild to moderate pain,
> Could well persuade me I'm an ancient wreck
> But here's what helps me to feel young again:
>   My love, who fell for me so long ago,
>   Still loves me just as much, and tells me so.

▪ Now read someone's attempt to classify what kind of poem it is.

1.	It's a poem
2.	It's a short personal poem, written in the first person expressing an idea or feeling (a lyric)
3.	It's a sonnet
4.	It's a Shakespearian sonnet
5.	It's an updated version of a Shakespearian sonnet, written in language that's simple and conversational
6.	It's quite a light-hearted poem but makes some serious points about love, time and ageing.

Broadly, this moves from bigger things, like what kind of poem it is, to the more precise and detailed things that make it special.

KS3 POETRY PLUS

- Pick any poem in the Anthology (pages 169-220) that you really like.

- Try to give your poem a classification, as if it were an animal. Start with the biggest thing about it and work down to more precise and specific things that *you* think make it special. Some of the aspects of poems that you might want to use in your classification are included below. Feel free to add others of your own!

- Give the poem a name as if it were a creature. For example, you might call Wendy Cope's poem 'Updated Shakespeare Look-a-Like'.

Classifying a poem

> - What broad category might it fit into? Here are some of the biggest divisions:
>   - A **narrative poem** – a poem that tells a story
>   - A **lyric poem** – a short poem that's personal and expresses an idea or feeling
>   - An **epic poem** – a great, long poem talking about heroic deeds
>   - An **ode** – a poem addressed to something or someone that you want to praise
>   - A **dramatic monologue** – a poem in the form of a long speech by someone, almost as if they're speaking in a play.

> - A poem written in a known form, with lots of rules (such as a **sonnet** or **haiku**) or a poem that is written in a much freer form (**free verse**)?

> - A personal, private poem or a poem written for a public audience?

> - A poem that works on the page or a poem that works in performance, spoken out loud?

> - A poem that is more conventionally poem-like or a poem that seems more everyday, or more like prose?

> - A poem that is highly **figurative** (uses metaphors or similes a lot) or a poem that is more **literal** (just describes things as they are, without lots of comparisons)?

> - A poem that is obviously part of a tradition or a poem that is very individual and unusual?

> - Anything else you notice that makes this poem special.

10 THINGS TO DO WITH AN ANTHOLOGY

4. Perform a Poem

- Work in small groups.

- Pick one poem from the Anthology (pages 169-220) that you think might lend itself to being performed. It might be good because:

    - It has different voices or dialogue
    - It has people in it, in particular places, so it conjures up a scene
    - It uses language in very patterned ways, so it could have different voices emphasising or echoing particular words or phrases
    - The tone is strong – emotional, powerful, angry or sad.

- When you have chosen a poem, you could prepare a performance of it for the rest of the class, in one of these three ways:

A. Create Still Pictures/Tableaux to Represent the Poem

- Select a moment or a series of moments from the poem and, in a group, create a series of frozen scenes. Have one person read the poem aloud, while the rest adopt their postures to go with particular lines or moments.

B. Turn the Poem Into a Dialogue/Script

- Create a playscript around the ideas, feelings and people in the poem, using words and phrases from it.

C. Perform a Reading

- Prepare a presentation of the poem using different voices, dramatic effects and sound effects if appropriate. You might include some of the effects listed below. Decide on which to use according to what you want to bring out in the poem.

    - Voices taking on different parts
    - More than one voice speaking at the same time to emphasise a word, phrase or repeated refrain
    - Loud and soft voices to bring out different moods in the poem
    - Actions or facial gestures to go with particular words or phrases
    - Spatial distances between the speakers (such as standing nearer or further apart, or standing, sitting, kneeling or lying down), depending on what's happening in the poem
    - Sound effects, such as hand clapping, clicking fingers, humming, a drum, a tambourine, a bell.

© ENGLISH & MEDIA CENTRE, 2018

KS3 POETRY PLUS

5. Blog About a Poem

Blogging about poems can be a great way to explore your ideas without having to worry about assessment – just having interesting conversations, with time to think and bounce your ideas off other people.

- Before you write your own blog, read the short blog below. It was written by a Year 7 pupil after she and her class had talked about a poem called 'This Poem':

> Hey everybody! It's Naomi-Lee here! Today I will be discussing my favourite poem called 'this poem'. This poem is so interesting and also very puzzling. I like this poem because it is funny and it is kind of like washing up detergent adverts because one of the lines in the poem is 'it should not be left within the reach of children, even adults'. It is very comedic and made me laugh the first time I read it. The thing that puzzles me about the poem is actually what another student, Kaiden, said which was 'is this really a poem?'. This made me wonder a little bit. Is it? This made me think in to my knowledge of poems and I came to the conclusion that I am in fact not sure and would like to hear another student's ideas to help decide mine. I like the end line 'words can seriously harm your heart'. I like this because in a way it is true. Poems do have an effect on your emotions which is one of the things I love about poems. They can take you away from society and the real world. Thank you for reading my response!

- As a class, share your response to this blog. What do you notice about the things Naomi-Lee chooses to write about and how she says them?

Writing a Blog of Your Own

- Three students will be given the task (or privilege!) of selecting one poem from the Anthology (pages 169-220) that you haven't yet studied as a class. It will be one that they are interested in, intrigued by or specially like. That poem will be the subject of a whole class blog.

- The three students should start off the blog by explaining which poem it is that they've chosen and why they selected it. They might also ask a few questions about the poem, or raise a few ideas. Here's what it might look like:

  ▶ We chose X as the poem because we like the way it…

  ▶ We wonder why…

  ▶ We're not sure what it means when it says…

  ▶ We think it might be…

10 THINGS TO DO WITH AN ANTHOLOGY

- Once the students have got the blog started, everyone else can start joining in for homework. You can respond to what other people say, try to answer each others' questions and generally talk to each other about the poem.

- At the end of the blogging period, hold a spoken 'summary' discussion in class to talk about:

  - What everyone now thinks about the poem
  - Which blog comments struck you as most interesting or persuasive
  - What you've learned by blogging in this way.

If you enjoyed this process, and felt you got a lot out of it, why not appoint three more people to choose a different poem and repeat the same process?

Blogging etiquette

Remember a blog is a public place, so you must:

- Be polite
- Avoid anything that might be offensive to anyone
- Argue with the ideas but not with the person
- Be positive and encouraging to everyone in your class – everyone has the right to their opinion
- Be aware that your teacher will be joining in, and looking at what you write.

© ENGLISH & MEDIA CENTRE, 2018

KS3 POETRY PLUS

6. The Random Poem Generator – Write a Poem

Instructions for the teacher

For this activity, you will need enough Random Poem Generator cards for every pupil to have three cards each. For most classes this means you will need two complete sets, chopped up. Put all the cards in a container or bag.

Pupil instructions

You are going to write a poem using some titles and phrases from poems in this book to get you started and give you ideas for the subject and style of the poem.

- Take it in turns to pull out three Random Poem Generator cards each, from the selection in the container your teacher will pass round. You might get a mixture of title and phrase cards, all phrase cards – or even all titles. It doesn't matter!

- Use one of your cards to write a poem of your own, using the word or phrase, either as the title, or as part of the poem itself. For an extra challenge, try using two of the cards. If you're feeling really brave, see if you can write something that works well using all three!

Title cards

The Schoolboy	Acquainted With the Night
No!	Butterfly
The Eagle	Time Does Not Bring Relief
How Do I Love Thee?	Animals
The Brain—is wider than the Sky—	Miss Charlotte Brown, Librarian, Goes Mad
Up-hill	Still I Rise
Autumn	Directions
Rain	The Instructions

10 THINGS TO DO WITH AN ANTHOLOGY

Phrase cards

| But to go to school in a summer morn, |

| No fruits, no flowers, no leaves, no birds, |

| The wrinkled sea |

| Let me count the ways. |

| A roof for when the slow dark hours begin. |

| I did not stop to speak, but nodded |

| Rain, midnight rain, nothing but the wild rain |

| I have looked down the saddest city lane. |

| Here in the garden, |

| I miss him in the weeping of the rain; |

KS3 POETRY PLUS

> The Brain is deeper than the sea—

> My small adventures

> I am afraid to lose you,

> like a syrupy sweet

> and suddenly I see a headline

> but we did have a few tricks up our sleeves

> alone, banana lies

> You may shoot me with your words,
> You may cut me with your eyes,

> from a past that's rooted in pain

> I know, it is a selfish thing.

10 THINGS TO DO WITH AN ANTHOLOGY

I will walk with you as far as

the symphony of tires, airplanes,
sirens, screams, engines –

I want you to know

Why not football
like everybody else /

into my back pocket

when I see a photograph

The night my mother tells the story of

after X Factor

- *Do not under any circumstances eat the angry man's sandwich*

KS3 POETRY PLUS

7. Write a Poem Based on a Poem

There are lots of fun ways of writing poems inspired by a poem you have read.

- Pick one poem in the Anthology (pages 169-220) that you really like.

- Think a bit about what you specially like about it. Make a bullet point list of those things, for example:
  - I like the way it makes me think about/feel…
  - I like its use of rhythm/rhyme/line breaks/metaphor…
  - I like the phrase….
  - It's special in the way it…

- Now try out *one* of these ways of writing a poem based on the one you've chosen. (Your teacher will tell you whether you have free choice or should do the one they suggest.)

A. Write a poem in the style of that poem

Look back at all the things you liked about the poem and try to write one of your own, on a different topic, in a really similar style. You could even have the same number of lines, the same shape and the same start.

B. Magpie poetry – stealing words and phrases

Pick out a maximum of six individual words or phrases that you specially like in the poem. Use as many of them as you like to write a completely new poem of your own, weaving them into your own poem.

D. Answering back to a poem

Some poems are addressed to someone else. The other person might have a different angle, or a set of things they would like to say in reply, for instance the loved one in Frank O' Hara's 'Animals' or in Wendy Cope's 'Sonnet'. Try answering back to the speaker of the poem.

Sometimes, a poem might not be directly addressed to someone but might be arguing a viewpoint on an issue or idea. Try answering back, with a poem of your own, that puts a different viewpoint on the same issue.

10 THINGS TO DO WITH AN ANTHOLOGY

D. 'The Golden Shovel' and other experiments

The golden shovel is a way of writing a poem invented by an American poet called Terrance Hayes, in which you take a line or lines from a favourite poem and make each word the last word of each line of your own poem.

So if you love the line 'So dawn goes down to dusk' from 'Nothing Gold Can Stay' by Robert Frost (page 189), your poem will be invented round these words, like this:

xxxxxxxxxxxxxxxxxxxxxxx **so**
xxxxxxxxxxxxxxxxxxxxxxx **dawn**
xxxxxxxxxxxxxxxxxxxxxxx **goes**
xxxxxxxxxxxxxxxxxxxxxxx **down**
xxxxxxxxxxxxxxxxxxxxxxx **to**
xxxxxxxxxxxxxxxxxxxxxxx **dusk.**

Here's how someone started a poem using these words:

> My brother expects everything in our bedroom to be just so
> He goes to bed late, listens to music, wakes me up at the crack of dawn

If this seems too hard, just use *some* of the words from your favourite line, or use *any* words from the poem you've chosen rather than just a single line.

Another shovel-like experiment

Here's a different kind of experiment, using just the final word of each line of W.B. Yeats' poem 'He Wishes for the Cloths of Heaven' (see page 184) to create a new poem. As you can see, you can end up with a poem that is very different from the original! See if you can write a poem of your own using all the last words of the lines of a favourite poem in this way.

> **I Wish For**
>
> You were always in the kitchen, mop in hand, cleaner, damp **cloths**
> You worked while Dad watched TV, even when it was no longer **light**
> You were the one who dressed us, wiped hands and faces with face **cloths**
> You got up early to get us to school, in the early morning, in the **half-light**
> You never complained, though we must have always been under your **feet**
> You listened to our stories, our silly thoughts and fears, our **dreams**
> You watched as we grew up, grew tall, left home, found our **feet**
> I never asked you about yourself, I never asked about your **dreams**.
>
> *Barbara Bleiman*

KS3 POETRY PLUS
8. Telling It Differently

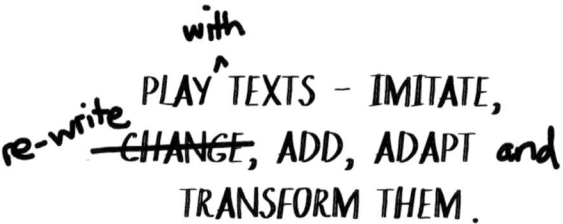

PLAY TEXTS with – IMITATE, re-write ~~CHANGE~~, ADD, ADAPT and TRANSFORM THEM.

Sometimes a poem can be a spark for writing in a different genre. For instance, some poems might work really well as a short story, a graphic novel, or a playscript.

▌ Flick through the collection of poems in the Anthology (pages 169-220) and choose one to transform into a different genre.

Here are a few examples to start you thinking about this:

- ▶ Turn the extract from *Beowulf* (page 170) into a chapter of a prose story for children
- ▶ Turn 'Acquainted with the Night' (page 190) into the opening of a short story
- ▶ Turn 'The Shortest and Sweetest of Songs' (page 181) into a short story
- ▶ Turn 'Politicians' (page 216) into a short 'Comment' piece in a newspaper.
- ▶ Turn 'The Way Through the Woods' (page 191) into a ghost story
- ▶ Turn 'The Schoolboy' (page 176) into a dialogue between a schoolboy or girl and a parent, in which the child argues why they should be allowed not to go to school.

10 THINGS TO DO WITH AN ANTHOLOGY

9. Create Your Own Mini-Anthology

- Using all the poems in the Anthology (pages 169-220), create your own little selection of five poems for each of these occasions:
    ▶ For a family member's birthday
    ▶ For next year's Year 7s
    ▶ For someone who doesn't much like poetry, or know much about it
    ▶ For one of your other teachers, for example your science or history teacher
    ▶ For keeping and looking back at when you've left school.

- Make a list of your selected titles, for each occasion, using the grid on page 26.

- Compare your choices with those of other people in the class. Discuss your reasons for choosing the ones you did.

- Pick one of your mini-collections. Actually create the anthology, by typing up the poems, putting illustrations with them, making a cover and writing an introduction to the collection.

- Display the collections in the class and give a copy of the collection to the person or people you created it for.

KS3 POETRY PLUS

	Poem 1	Poem 2	Poem 3	Poem 4	Poem 5
For a family member's birthday					
For next year's Year 7s					
For someone who doesn't much like poetry					
For one of your other teachers, e.g. your Science or History teacher					
For keeping and looking back at, when you've left school					

10 THINGS TO DO WITH AN ANTHOLOGY

10. Do a Poetry Investigation

Try this activity after you've completed some of the other units and activities in this book. It allows you to *apply* some of what you've learned, using all the poems in the Anthology (pages 169-220).

You could do just one of these activities and spend a good long stretch of time on it, perhaps coming back to do another one on another occasion. Or you could do lots of them at speed, all at once, in one lesson. A good long stretch is good for doing a detailed investigation, in small groups. Doing lots at speed is good for thinking fast and thinking on your feet. Your teacher will tell you which to do.

- Work either in pairs, groups, or on your own.

> ### A. PATTERNS AND STRUCTURE IN POEMS
>
> - Find one poem in the Anthology (pages 169-220) that seems to you to do each of the following:
>   - Sets up a pattern at the beginning that is changed by the end
>   - Has a pattern (such as a refrain, or a repeated start of each line) that keeps on being repeated right the way through the poem
>   - Has a pattern (such as a refrain, or a repeated start of each line) that keeps on being repeated right the way through the poem but with a small change in the middle of the poem or at the end
>   - Starts happily and finishes sadly
>   - Starts sadly and finishes happily
>   - Falls into two parts
>   - Falls into three or more parts
>   - Has a different structure that interests you.
> - Pick one of these poems – the one with the structure that interests you most. Work out your thoughts about the structure, how it works and what you like about it.
> - Share your ideas in a small group, or with the rest of the class.

KS3 POETRY PLUS

B. PUNCTUATION

- Find one poem in the Anthology (pages 169-220) that seems to you to do each of the following:
    - Uses punctuation in an unusual or surprising way
    - Has no punctuation
    - Uses punctuation in a fairly predictable way.

- Pick one of these poems – the one with the punctuation that interests you most. Work out your thoughts about the use of punctuation, how it works, what difference it makes to the poem and what you like about it.

- Share your ideas in a small group, or with the rest of the class.

C. LINES, LINE BREAKS AND LOOK ON THE PAGE

- Find one poem in the Anthology (pages 169-220) in which:
    - A single line stands out from all the others
    - The lines break at a different place to where you'd expect them to
    - The lines run on, with whole sentences covering several lines (the technical term for this is enjambment)
    - The lines are all very similar in length
    - The lines are quite different lengths
    - The poem is set out on the page in an unexpected, unusual way.

- Pick one of these poems – the one that you think uses lines or line breaks in the most interesting way. Think about something to say about what's specially interesting about the lines or line breaks.

- Share your ideas in a small group, or with the rest of the class.

10 THINGS TO DO WITH AN ANTHOLOGY

D. IMAGERY – METAPHORS, SIMILES, SYMBOLS

- Find one poem in the Anthology (pages 169-220) in which:
  - A single image (metaphor, simile or symbol) is developed over the whole poem
  - Several metaphors or similes are developed across the poem
  - Everything is very literal – nothing stands for (represents) something else
  - The poem is playful, using metaphors and similes in comic ways
  - The poem uses unusual metaphors to make its point.
- Pick one of these poems – the one that you think uses imagery in the most interesting way. Think about something to say about what's specially interesting about the use of imagery.
- Share your ideas in a small group, or with the rest of the class.

E. VOICE AND VOICES

- Find one poem in the Anthology (pages 169-220) in which:
  - The voice is first person (I)
  - The voice is third person (he/she/they)
  - The poem is addressed to someone else (you)
  - The poem contains dialogue between people
  - The voice is very personal and intimate
  - The voice is public and impersonal
  - The voice is strident and strong
  - The voice is light-hearted and amusing.
- Pick one of these poems – the one where you find the voice most interesting. Think about something to say about what's specially interesting to you about how voice is used in that poem.
- Share your ideas in a small group, or with the rest of the class.

© ENGLISH & MEDIA CENTRE, 2018

F. MOOD, TONE, FEELING

- Find one poem in the Anthology (pages 169-220) in which:
  - The mood is sad, regretful, unhappy
  - The mood is happy, upbeat, light-hearted
  - The mood is thoughtful, reflective
  - The mood is angry
  - The mood is peaceful, quiet.
- Pick one of these poems – the one where you find the mood most interesting, or best conveyed. Think about something to say about what's specially interesting about how it's conveyed and its effect on you as a reader.
- Share your ideas in a small group, or with the rest of the class.

G. SOUND, RHYTHM AND RHYME

- Find one poem in the Anthology (pages 169-220) in which:
  - The rhythm seems to echo the meaning
  - The rhythm helps set up a pattern that is memorable or song-like
  - The rhythm is broken somewhere, in a way that links to a change in tone or ideas
  - The sounds of the words connect to the ideas, feelings or things described
  - Rhyming words draw attention to important things, or connect with each other
  - Words that only half rhyme, or rhymes that are expected and aren't given, make you notice them particularly.
- Pick one of these poems – the one where you find the use of sound most interesting. Think of something to say about what's specially interesting to you about how sound is used in that poem.
- Share your ideas in a small group, or with the rest of the class.

WORDS
FORM
PERFORMANCE
SOUND
RHYME
WHAT IS A POEM?

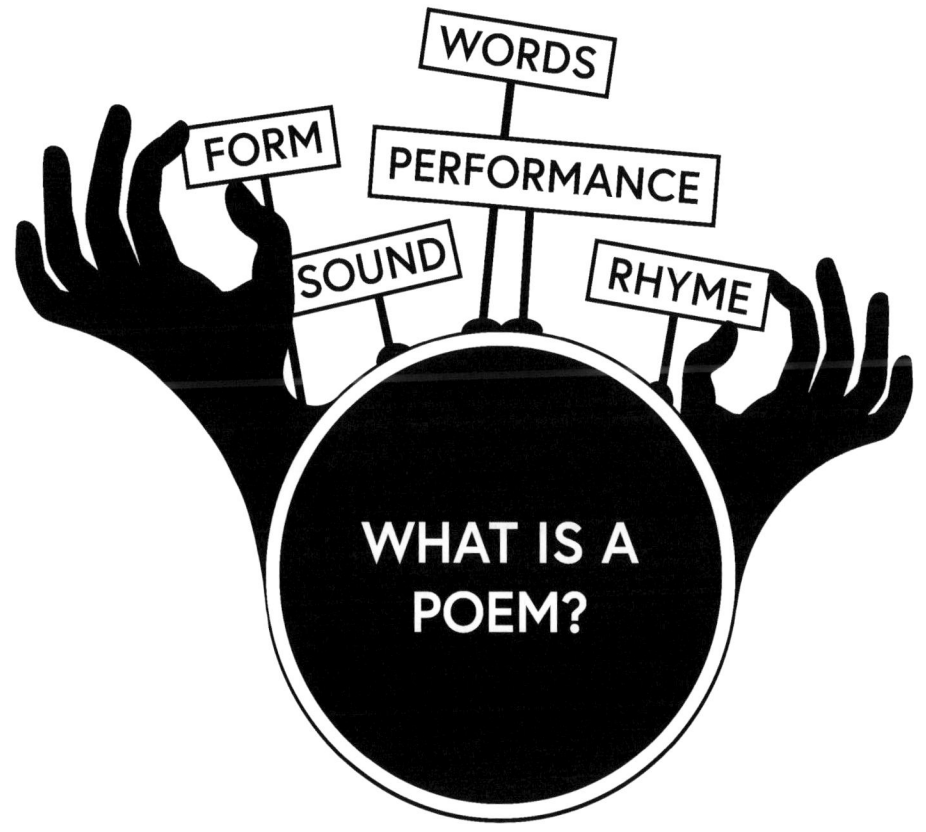

KS3 POETRY PLUS

WHAT IS A POEM?

> In this unit you are going to think about what makes a poem a *poem*. You will read a range of different texts that might or might not be thought of as poetry, before exploring your own personal criteria for what you like and what makes good poetry.

Investigating What a Poem Is

There are no hard and fast rules about what makes a poem. There are ingredients that are common to lots of poems, such as:

- Rhyme
- Layout in lines and verses
- Playful or imaginative use of language
- Regular rhythm
- Imagery such as metaphors and similes
- Repetition of words or phrases or whole lines.

But none of these are absolutely essential to any single poem. A poem can exist perfectly well without using any of them. So what *exactly* makes a poem a poem?

To help you start to think about what a poem is, you are going to read a selection of texts that are poems, extracts from poems – or not poems at all!

- In groups, read each text in turn and discuss whether or not you think it is a poem, or an extract from a poem.
  - If you think it is a poem, jot down reasons why, for example: it rhymes; it uses line breaks in interesting ways; it is thought-provoking.
  - If you think it isn't a poem, try to explain why.
- Share your thinking in whole class discussion.

When you have finished your discussions, your teacher will tell you where each text came from – and whether or not it was originally published as a poem*.

- Talk about anything that surprises you. What have you discovered about what poetry is?

* Answers in the Appendix.

WHAT IS A POEM?

1	**4.** Settled in the bowl alone, banana lies there cuddle-curved, waiting.

2	When he woke in the woods in the dark and the cold of the night he'd reach out to touch the child sleeping beside him. Nights dark beyond darkness and the days more gray each one than what had gone before.

3	a day so hot that sand could boil to glass she, a striped cat who purrs he, a tamed bear.

4	Old houses were scaffolding once and workmen whistling.

5	Sssnnnwhufffll? Hnwhuffl hhnnwfl hnfl hfl? Gdroblboblhobngbl gbl gl g g g g glbgl. Drublhaflablhaflubhafgabhaflhafl fl fl – gm grawwwww grf grawf awfgm graw gm. Hovoplodok-doplodovok-plovodokot-doplodokosh?

6	Colds are caused by viruses and easily spread to other people. You're infectious until all your symptoms have gone. This usually takes a week or two. Colds are spread by germs from coughs and sneezes which can live on hands and surfaces for 24 hours. To reduce the risk of spreading a cold: • wash your hands often with warm water and soap • use tissues to trap germs when you cough or sneeze • bin used tissues as quickly as possible.

7	Here lies John Bun, He was killed by a gun, His name was not Bun, it was Wood, But Wood would not rhyme with gun, but Bun would.

8	Glory be to God for dappled things –
	    For skies of couple-colour as a brinded cow;
	      For rose-moles all in stipple upon trout that swim;
	Fresh-firecoal chestnut-falls; finches' wings;
	    Landscape plotted and pieced – fold, fallow, and plough;

9	Ye cannae shove yer granny aff a bus, Oh ye cannae shove yer granny aff a bus, Ye cannae shove yer granny, for she's yer mammy's mammy, Ye cannae shove yer granny aff a bus.

WHAT IS A POEM?

10

The night is darkening round me,
The wild winds coldly blow;
But a tyrant spell has bound me,
And I cannot, cannot go.

The giant trees are bending
Their bare boughs weighed with snow;
The storm is fast descending,
And yet I cannot go.

11

5. If you do not follow THE INSTRUCTIONS

You will likely face some tricky moments. Apologies for this.
However, there is also a good chance that something

strangeexcitingremarkableunexpectedslightly-
frighteningbutbrightlycoloured

will happen.

12

Queen Jane lay in labour full nine days or more,
Till the women were so tired, they could stay no longer there,

'Good women, good women, good women as ye be,
Do open my right side and find my baby.'

'Oh no,' said the women. 'That never may be,
We will send for King Henry, and hear what he say.'

| 13 | What can a yellow glove mean in a world of motorcars and governments?

I was small, like everyone. Life was a string of precautions: Don't kiss the squirrel before you bury him, don't suck candy, pop balloons, drop watermelons, watch TV. When the new gloves appeared one Christmas, tucked in soft tissue, I heard it trailing me: Don't lose the yellow gloves. |

| 14 | Come
Home. |

| 15 | I am the dream and the hope of the slave.
I rise
I rise
I rise. |

| 16 | A Mars a day helps you work, rest and play. |

WHAT IS A POEM?

What Do You Like in a Poem?

- Working on your own, flick through the Anthology (pages 169-220) and choose a poem you like.

- Still working on your own, practise reading your poem aloud and think about why you like it. You don't have to understand it or be able to explain it – you may like it because it makes you puzzle and think!

- Working in a small group, listen as each person reads their poem aloud and explains why they chose it.

- After listening to all the poems and talking about why you like them, compile a list in your group called: **What We Like About Poems**.

- Share your thinking about what you like about poems as a class. See if you can come up with at least ten points between you. It doesn't matter if these contradict each other, for example one person may prefer poems that rhyme, whereas someone else may prefer poems that don't.

What Is Poetry? Drawing on the Experts

- In a pair or small groups, read the quotations on page 38 which show what some poets think poetry is.

- Place them in rank order in terms of which you find most to least interesting.

- Discuss your group's order and thinking with the rest of the class.

KS3 POETRY PLUS

Poets on poetry

| A | Of the many definitions of poetry, the simplest is still the best: 'memorable speech'.
W.H. Auden |

| B | Thoughts that breathe, and words that burn.
Thomas Gray |

| C | Poetry is a deal of joy and pain and wonder, with a dash of the dictionary.
Kahlil Gibran |

| D | Poetry's like a huge multi-coloured marquee that has room for all kinds of forms and voices.
Vicki Feaver |

| E | Sir, what is Poetry? Why, Sir, it is much easier to say what it is not. We all know what light is: but it is not easy to tell what it is.
Samuel Johnson |

| F | If I read a book and it makes my whole body so cold no fire can warm me, I know that is poetry. If I feel physically as if the top of my head were taken off, I know that is poetry. These are the only way I know it. Is there any other way?
Emily Dickinson |

| G | Poetry is eternal graffiti written in the heart of everyone.
Lawrence Ferlinghetti |

| H | Poetry, therefore, we will call Musical Thought.
Thomas Carlyle |

| I | Prose = words in their best order; poetry = the best words in their best order.
Samuel Taylor Coleridge |

WHAT IS A POEM?

What Makes a Good Poem?

You have considered what makes a poem a poem and what you like about poems. Now you are going to work with a partner to draw up some criteria for what makes a good poem. You can use ideas that came up in previous activities, or decide on new ones.

- Working with your partner, agree on five criteria that, in your opinion, make a good poem, for example it makes readers look at the world in unusual ways.

- Write your criteria on a chart like the one on page 40.

- Look through the poems in the Anthology (pages 169-220). Choose two poems each. Choose them randomly rather than looking for ones that you like.

- Read the four poems together, reading each one twice.

- For each of your five criteria, give the poem a score as follows: 0 = doesn't meet this criterion at all; 5 = a fantastic example of this criterion

- Add up your scores to see which poem fulfils your criteria best. Discuss whether this is in fact the poem that you like best.

- Review your criteria, using the questions below to help you:

  ▶ Which of your criteria might you want to change as a result of this activity? For example, a poem that you didn't particularly like may have scored highly and this might make you re-think your criteria.

  ▶ Which criteria might you want to add as a result of this activity? For example, you may have particularly liked a poem with a strong rhythm but not have anything on your criteria about rhythm.

- Share your thinking as a class.

KS3 POETRY PLUS

What makes a good poem?

Criteria for what makes a good poem	Poem 1 Score 0 - 5	Poem 2 Score 0 - 5	Poem 3 Score 0 - 5	Poem 4 Score 0 - 5
1.				
2.				
3.				
4.				
5.				

WHAT IS A POEM?

What Is a Poem? On Reflection…

In this unit you have read a number of different poems and thought about what poems are, based on your own ideas and those of a range of poets. This final activity gives you the opportunity to reflect on the work you have done, as well as summarising some ideas that might be useful when working through the rest of *KS3 Poetry Plus*.

- In a small group create a Diamond 9 pattern using the statements on page 42, placing the statement you agree with most at the top. You will have discussed ideas like this when working your way through the unit, but there might be new ones too.

- Discuss your Diamond 9 formation with the rest of the class, explaining your decisions.

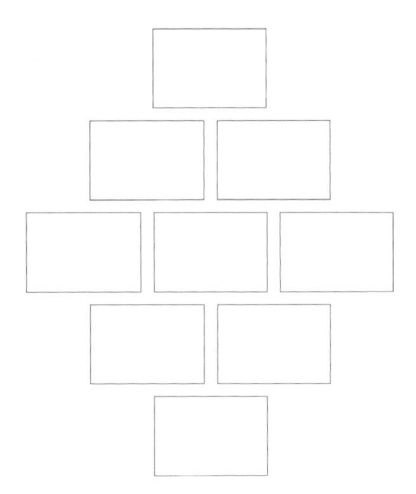

Pulling Together Your Thinking

- On your own, choose a poem from the Anthology (pages 169-220) that you particularly like. Write a few paragraphs about this poem, focusing on:
  - What you like about it
  - What makes it a poem
  - What makes it a good poem
  - How it fits in with the ideas you have explored in this unit.

(As an alternative, you might like to write a poem of your own and write about it in the same way – what you like about it, what makes it good, and so on.)

KS3 POETRY PLUS

What is a poem? Statements for a Diamond 9

A. Poems are poems because of where you read or hear them. If someone says something is a poem and puts it in a book, or reads it at a performance, then it is a poem.

B. Poems have a particular kind of layout, for example using line breaks, verses, traditional forms, interesting shapes, etc.

C. Poems use lots of figurative language (words or expressions with a meaning different from the literal) such as metaphor, simile, personification, hyperbole.

D. Poems have a strong emotional impact on readers.

E. Poems express ideas and feelings in a very condensed form.

F. Poems make readers look at the world in unusual ways.

G. Poems use memorable vocabulary.

H. Poems use patterned language – patterns made and patterns broken.

I. Poems show the possibilities of language.

SAY IT OUT LOUD!

KS3 POETRY PLUS

SAY IT OUT LOUD!

> In this unit you will consider the oral traditions in which so much of poetry is rooted. You will think about early spoken poetry, how important it was for it to be memorable for listeners and how this has influenced all poetry that has followed. You will develop an oral poem of your own and explore the modern tradition of poetry slams. In doing this you will have the opportunity to think carefully about:
>
> - The role of sound in poetry
> - The links between poetry and story telling
> - What makes poetry distinct from other forms of language use
> - The role of performance in poetry.

What Makes Spoken Poetry Memorable?

Poetry pre-dates literacy. In other words, people were reciting and listening to poems before the establishment of writing. It is believed that the earliest poetry was recited or sung as a way of remembering things of importance: history, traditions, the law, and so on.

In a way this is still the case. As children we learn nursery rhymes, which might be regarded as a type of poetry, before we can read and write. We do this partly because they are fun to listen to and say out loud, but also as part of the process of learning language and learning about the world.

Early poetry and nursery rhymes both use language in particular ways to help people remember them. This is important. Without being remembered, the messages in these texts would simply disappear.

The following activities, then, are designed to get you thinking about what helps to make oral poetry memorable and how some of these things have become an important part of all poetry.

SAY IT OUT LOUD!

What Do You Remember?

- Discuss in small groups examples of nursery rhymes, songs, skipping or other games, songs and poems that you know off by heart.

- Take it in turns to say out loud one of the examples that you remember. As you are speaking, the other members in your group should listen out for what makes it easy to remember, for example a regular rhyme scheme.

- Make a list of all the things that made your examples easy to remember.

Memorable Speech

- Poet W.H. Auden said that poetry was 'memorable speech'. On your own, look at the Anthology on pages 169 to 220 and choose one poem of more than four lines that you think is memorable speech.

- Read your poem to your partner and explain why you think it is memorable.

- Share some of your poems and reasons as a class.

- Return to the list you made for the previous activity. Add to it any additional information from this activity about what makes a poem memorable, if read aloud.

What Is Most Important?

On page 46 is a list of what might make a poem memorable, if read aloud.

- In pairs, go through the list and identify anything that you did not think of for the previous two activities. Do the additional points apply in any way to the poems you have been discussing?

- Now rank order the list with what you think most helps make a poem memorable at the top.

- Discuss your different orders as a whole class.

KS3 POETRY PLUS

What is most important?

A. Has a regular rhythm

B. Uses unusual words or phrases

C. Contains repeated words and phrases

D. Uses interesting images

E. Uses a regular rhyme scheme

F. Uses lists

G. Is written in a familiar form, for example a ballad, a limerick

H. Uses words and phrases that regularly appear in everyday life

I. Uses alliteration and other forms of sound patterning

J. Speaks directly to the listener as 'you' or 'we'

K. Uses short sentences

L. Uses formulaic phrases that everyone recognises, for example 'Once upon a time', 'I'll tell you a story'

SAY IT OUT LOUD!

Beowulf – A Heroic Tale

Beowulf is a very early poem from the 11th-century AD, perhaps one of the first ever to be written down in English. In those days, English was called Anglo-Saxon. It was very different to modern English. It has some familiar words but lots of unfamiliar ones too. *Beowulf* is a tale of heroism and valour, which tells of how the hero, Beowulf, comes to the aid of the King of the Danes, to save his community from a dreadful monster who is threatening to murder them all. Scholars believe that the version we can now read was probably told orally by many different poets, over many decades before it was finally written down.

Alliterative Verse – Designed for Speaking and Performing

Beowulf was spoken (and later written) in a kind of verse called 'alliterative verse'. The rhythm of the lines comes from repeating the same sound several times in each line. It has the big advantage of being easy to remember because of the repeated vowel or consonant sound. Many Anglo-Saxon poems were spoken and then written down using this kind of rhythm.

Here's an example, the opening of a poem called *Piers Plowman*, in Anglo-Saxon followed by two translations, one a literal English translation that keeps the alliteration, the other a more modern one.

> ### Original Anglo-Saxon
> *A feir feld full of folk || fond I þer bitwene,*
> *Of alle maner of men, || þe mene and þe riche,*
> *Worchinge and wandringe || as þe world askeþ.*

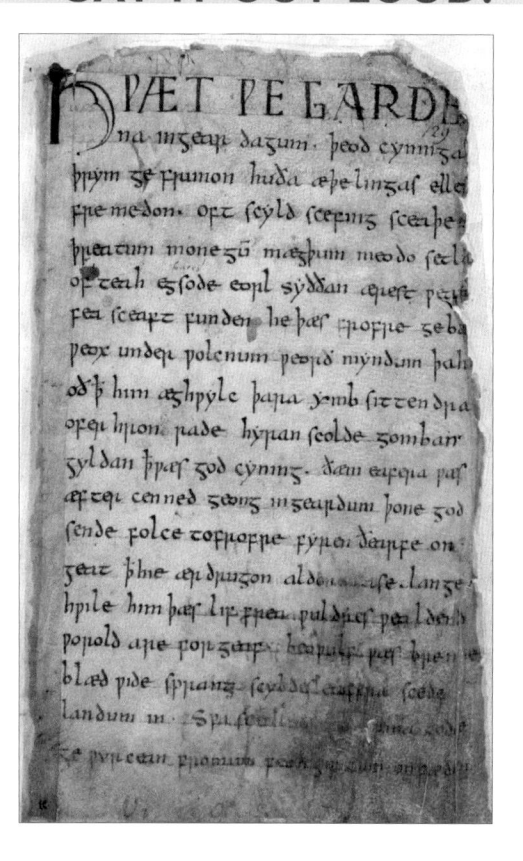

KS3 POETRY PLUS

1	**A Literal Translation** A fair field full of folk found I there between Of all manner of men, the mean and the rich Working and wandering, as the world asks.

2	**A Modern Translation** Among them I came across a field crowded with people All kinds of men, the poor and the rich Going about their business and walking around, as the world expects of them.

An Experiment

Try this little experiment. Half the class should try to learn the literal translation and the other half should try to learn the modern one. You have just five minutes.

- Now put the poems to one side and pair up with someone who had a different translation to you. Each try to say as much as you can of the version you learned.

- As a class discuss who learned the poem more easily. Which poem do you think was easiest to learn? What does that tell you about alliterative verse?

Here's another published modern translation that tries to keep the alliteration for a modern audience.

3	**Another Modern Translation** Among them I found a fair field full of people All manner of men, the poor and the rich Working and wandering as the world requires.

- Talk about which of the three translations you like best and why.

SAY IT OUT LOUD!

The Monster Grendel Threatens the Danes – An Alliterative Verse Translation

Included on page 50 are two extracts from *Beowulf*. They tell of how Grendel the monster came to murder the Danes, in their 'hall', where the king and his followers lived.

You'll need to know seven words that aren't modern, to get the gist of the extract. Other words you can probably guess at, or ask your teacher to explain.

> ▶ **A march-riever** is someone who walks or haunts the borderlands
> ▶ **A wight** is a person
> ▶ **A fastness** is a secure, fortified place
> ▶ **A fief** is a piece of land owned and controlled by someone
> ▶ **An atheling** is a prince or lord
> ▶ **A thane** is a nobleman
> ▶ **Wassailing** means drinking lots of ale and having a good time.

- In pairs or small groups, try reading the extracts aloud. Read both several times, trying to get familiar enough with them to be able to make it a real performance, with all the fear and excitement of the story of a monster threatening a community.

- Listen to some of the performances, as a whole class.

- Now look more closely at the lines. Work out which vowel or consonant drives the rhythm of each line. For instance, in the first line it seems to be the 'g' in 'Grendel' and 'grim'.

- Try writing the next two or three lines of the poem, in which you choose a sound to drive the rhythm of each of your lines and repeat it at least three times.

Writing Your Own Poem in Alliterative Verse

- Have a go at writing a very short poem of your own – no more than 6 lines – using alliterative verse. You could write about your journey to school each day, or your favourite foods, or a poem about your school subjects or your own tale of adventure and monsters.

- Choose a different sound to repeat in each line. Here's an example line to show you how it might work:

    On Mondays it's Maths making my mind buzz in multiple ways

    On Tuesdays....etc.

KS3 POETRY PLUS

Extract 1

Grendel this monster grim was called,
march-riever mighty, in moorland living,
in fen and fastness; fief of the giants
the hapless wight a while had kept
since the Creator his exile doomed.

Extract 2

Went he forth to find at fall of night
that haughty house, and heed wherever
the Ring-Danes, outrevelled, to rest had gone.
Found within it the atheling band
asleep after feasting and fearless of sorrow,
of human hardship. Unhallowed wight,
grim and greedy, he grasped betimes,
wrathful, reckless, from resting-places,
thirty of the thanes, and thence he rushed
fain of his fell spoil, faring homeward,
laden with slaughter, his lair to seek.
Then at the dawning, as day was breaking,
the might of Grendel to men was known;
then after wassail was wail uplifted,
loud moan in the morn. The mighty chief,
atheling excellent, unblithe sat,
laboured in woe for the loss of his thanes,
when once had been traced the trail of the fiend,
spirit accurst: too cruel that sorrow,
too long, too loathsome. Not late the respite;
with night returning, anew began
ruthless murder; he recked no whit,
firm in his guilt, of the feud and crime.

Anon, translated by Francis B. Grummere

SAY IT OUT LOUD!

Passing Down Stories – Creating a Spoken and a Written Poem From Memory

A folk tale is reproduced below and on pages 52-53. It is not there for you to read, though, but for your teacher. They will read it before the lesson, then either read it to you is as it is written, or, better still, they will try to retell it from memory. (You might want to give them some guidance about how to do this, such as writing down key moments to remember, memorising key phrases that stand out, presenting confidently, using a clear, engaging voice, and so on!)

- You should have this book closed while your teacher does the retelling. (Even if they decide simply to read the story from the book, you should have your copy closed and resist reading it yourself.)

The Woman of the Sea

One clear summer night, a young man was walking on the sand by the sea on the Isle of Unst. He had been all day in the hayfields and was come down to the shore to cool himself, for it was the full moon and the wind blowing fresh off the water.

As he came to the shore he saw the sand shining white in the moonlight and on it the sea-people dancing. He had never seen them before, for they show themselves like seals by day, but on this night, because it was midsummer and a full moon, they were dancing for joy. Here and there he saw dark patches where they had flung down their sealskins, but they themselves were as clear as the moon itself, and they cast no shadow.

He crept a little nearer, and his own shadow moved before him, and of a sudden one of the sea-people danced upon it. The dance was broken. They looked about and saw him and with a cry they fled to their sealskins and dived into the waves. The air was full of their soft crying and splashing.

But one of the fairy people ran hither and thither on the sands, wringing her hands as if she had lost something. The young man looked and saw a patch of darkness in his own shadow. It was a seal's skin. Quickly he threw it behind a rock and watched to see what the sea-fairy would do.

She ran down to the edge of the sea and stood with her feet in the foam, crying to her people to wait for her, but they had gone too far to hear. The moon shone on her and the young man thought she was the loveliest creature he had even seen. Then she began to weep softly to herself and the sound of it was so pitiful that he could bear it no longer. He stood upright and went down to her.

'What have you lost, woman of the sea?' he asked her.

She turned at the sound of his voice and looked at him, terrified. For a moment he thought she was going to dive into the sea. Then she came a step nearer and held up her two hands to him.

'Sir,' she said, 'give it back to me, and I and my people will give you the treasure of the sea.' Her voice was like the waves singing in a shell.

'I would rather have you than the treasure of the sea,' said the young man. Although she hid her face in her hands and fell again to crying, more hopeless than ever, he was not moved.

'It is my wife you shall be,' he said. 'Come with me now to the priest, and we will go home to our own house, and it is yourself shall be mistress of all I have. It is warm you will be in the long winter nights, sitting at your own hearth stone and the peat burning red, instead of swimming in the cold green sea.'

She tried to tell him of the bottom of the sea where there come neither snow nor darkness of night and the waves are as warm as a river in summer, but he would not listen. Then he threw his cloak around her and lifted her in his arms and they were married in the priest's house.

He brought her home to his little thatched cottage and into the kitchen with its earthen floor, and set her down before the hearth in the red glow of the peat. She cried out when she saw the fire, for she thought it was a strange crimson jewel.

'Have you anything as bonny as that in the sea?' he asked her, kneeling down beside her and she said, so faintly that he could scarcely hear her, 'No.'

'I know not what there is in the sea,' he said, 'but there is nothing on land as bonny as you.' For the first time she ceased her crying and sat looking into the heart of the fire. It was the first thing that made her forget, even for a moment, the sea which was her home.

All the days she was in the young man's house, she never lost the wonder of the fire and it was the first thing she brought her children to see. For she had three children in the twice seven years she lived with him. She was a good wife to him. She baked his bread and she spun the wool from the fleece of his Shetland sheep.

He never named the seal's skin to her, nor she to him, and thought she was content, for he loved her dearly and she was happy with her children. Once, when he was ploughing on the headland above the bay, he looked down and saw her standing on the rocks and crying in a mournful voice to a great seal in the water. He said nothing when she came home, for he thought to himself it was not to wonder at if she were lonely for the sight of her own people. As for the seal's skin, he had hidden it well.

There came a September evening and she was busy in the house, and the children playing hide-and-seek in the stacks in the gloaming. She heard them shouting and went out to them.

'What have you found?' she said.

The children came running to her. 'It is like a big cat,' they said, 'but it is softer than a cat. Look!' she looked and saw her seal's skin that was hidden under last year's hay.

She gazed at it, and for a long time she stood still. It was warm dusk and the air was yellow with the afterglow of the sunset. The children had run away again, and their voices among the stacks sounded like the voices of birds. The hens were on the roost already and now and then one of them clucked in its sleep. The air was full of little friendly noises from the sleepy talking of the swallows under the thatch. The door was open and the warm smell of the baking of bread came out to her.

She turned to go in, but a small breath of wind rustled over the stacks and she stopped again. It brought a sound that she had heard so long she never seemed to hear it at all. It was the sea whispering down on the sand. Far out on the rocks the great waves broke in a boom, and close in on the sand the little waves slipped racing back. She took up the seal's skin and went swiftly down the track that led to the sands. The children saw her and cried to her to wait for them, but she did not hear them. She was just out of sight when their father came in from the byre and they ran to tell him.

'Which road did she take?' said he.

'The low road to the sea,' they answered, but already their father was running to the shore. The children tried to follow him, but their voices died away behind him, so fast did he run.

As he ran across the hard sands, he saw her dive to join the big seal who was waiting for her, and he gave a loud cry to stop her. For a moment she rested on the surface of the sea, then she cried with her voice that was like the waves singing in a shell, 'Fare ye well, and all good befall you, for you were a good man to me.'

Then she dived to the fairy places that lie at the bottom of the sea and the big seal with her.

For a long time her husband watched for her to come back to him and the children; but she came no more.

KS3 POETRY PLUS

Writing a Poem – A Key Scene

Stage 1: Make a tableau

- In groups of four, create a tableau (a still picture) about one key scene that you remember from the story you have just heard. This will take you about five minutes.

- Take it in turns to present your tableau to the rest of the class. As you freeze into position, your classmates should jot down the following:
  - A title for your tableau
  - The scene they think is being shown
  - Words and phrases that come to mind
  - Questions, thoughts, ideas that come to mind.

Stage 2: Create a spoken poem

- When you have each shown your tableau, share your notes with your original group. Select one tableau that really made you think hard, or that you really liked.

- Your next task is to turn this into an oral poem. To make this into a real challenge, you must develop it without writing your poem out in full. You can, however, jot down words and phrases to help you. Here are some things to consider:
  - Will your poem use repeated lines or words?
  - Will your poem use rhyme?
  - Will your poem use alliteration?
  - Will you use any words or phrases that you specially like, or remember from your teacher's telling of the story?
  - How much will you require each member of your group to remember?
  - Are there any words or lines that all of you will deliver?

- Practise saying your poem out loud as a group, then take it in turns to perform it in front of the rest of your class.

- When you have all finished, discuss as a class:
  - Any words and phrases that leapt out at you, that you specially enjoyed and why
  - What helped you remember your poems, what the experience was of delivering them
  - What it was like to listen to them.

Stage 3: Create a written poem

Poems on the page often draw on the oral elements of performance but they also add other elements. The way it is set out on the page can make a poem memorable for a reader and emphasise particular words or ideas, just as the spoken effects can make it memorable to listen to.

You're going to work on your own to write a poem that draws on the poem you have just presented out loud.

- Write a poem that looks good on the page. Write it afresh – don't just copy the spoken poem you did as a group. To do this, experiment with:
  - The order of the words and phrases you choose
  - Where you choose to break the lines
  - Where you choose to start a new verse.
- When you have finished, compare your written poems with other members of your original group and discuss the different choices you have made.

Stage 4: A published poet's version of 'The Woman of the Sea'

A poem by Seamus Heaney based on the story of 'The Woman of the Sea' is included on page 56.

- Read the poem with a partner and discuss the following:
  - What first thoughts do you have about Heaney's poem? Are there things you specially liked, or found interesting compared with your own?
  - Which lines do you find interesting because of what they say?
  - Which lines do you find interesting because of how they sound?
  - Which three words or phrases would you steal to put in your own?
- Share your thoughts as a whole class.
- Return to your own written poem and work on it to improve on the original in any way that you like. You might borrow some of Heaney's words, take inspiration from some of the ways he wrote, or simply use ideas of your own.

Stage 5: Reflection

- Write out your final poem. Alongside it write a short reflective piece about:
  - Which lines in your poem you think are most interesting
  - What you most like about the way your poem sounds
  - What you learned from writing a poem in this way – from spoken to written, learning from a published poet, redrafting your poem.

Maighdean Mara

For Séan Oh-Eocha

I

She sleeps now, her cold breasts
Dandled by undertow,
Her hair lifted and laid.
Undulant slow seawracks
Cast about shin and thigh,
Bangles of wort, drifting
Liens catch, dislodge gently.

This is the great first sleep
Of homecoming, eight
Land years between hearth and
Bed, steeped and dishevelled.
Her magic garment al-
most ocean-tinctured still.

II

He stole her garment as
She combed her hair: follow
Was all that she could do.
He hid it in the eaves
And charmed her there, four walls,
Warm floor, man-love nightly
In earshot of the waves.

She suffered milk and birth—
She had no choice—conjured
Patterns of home and drained
The tidesong from her voice
Then the thatcher came and stuck
Her garment in a stack.
Children carried tales back.

III

In night air, entering
Foam, she wrapped herself
With smoke-reeks from his thatch,
Straw-musts and films of mildew.
She dipped his secret there
Forever and uncharmed

Accents of fisher wives,
The dead hold of bedrooms,
Dread of the night and morrow,
Her children's brush and combs.
She sleeps now, her cold breasts
Dandled by undertow.

Seamus Heaney

SAY IT OUT LOUD!

A Virtual Poetry Slam

There is still a strong tradition of poets performing live, speaking poems rather than reading them, sometimes with music. In the 1980s in Chicago and New York, the people who put on open mic events, when anyone could get up and read their work, decided to make them more exciting for the audience by turning them into a competition called a 'Poetry Slam'. In slams, members of the audience are chosen to act as judges for the evening. Slams have grown in popularity and there are now both European and World Poetry Slam championships. There are also many slams for young people, with prizes for champion slammers.

You are going to hold your own, virtual, poetry slam where you are the judges.

- As a class, follow the links to watch the following poets on video performing a poem, or watch others chosen by your teacher:

On the EMC website (see page 5 for details):
- Harry Baker: 'I've Got 99 Problems'
- Caleb Femi: 'Fam'
- Michael Rosen: 'The Book'.

On YouTube:
- Kate Tempest: 'Circles' https://www.youtube.com/watch?v=vM09uPsvWIM
- Ernestine Johnson: 'Formation' https://www.youtube.com/watch?v=6Xnuya263iM

- As a class, watch the poets again. After each poem, make a few notes for yourself about what you enjoyed about both the poem and the performance, as well as anything you did not like.

- As a class, discuss anything the poets did to make their poems memorable. You can draw on ideas explored earlier in this unit.

- Get into groups of three and watch the poets again. Agree on two scores (marks out of 10) for each poet: one for the poem and one for the performance. Be ready to explain reasons for your scores.

- Hear from several groups around the class and listen to the reasons they give for their scores.

- Add up all the group scores to find the winner of your virtual poetry slam.

- If you wish you could also have a free vote where each person votes for their personal winner, regardless of what the rest of their group think.

KS3 POETRY PLUS
Pulling It All Together – One Final Performance

You are now going to draw on everything you have learned about how poetry works as a spoken form to put on a class poetry slam of your own. You can work on your own poem for the slam, as a pair, or in a group.

Your teacher will tell you how the slam will be judged – either by the loudness of clapping or by a panel of judges chosen from members of the class.

Here's a list of four options for a poem for the slam but if you have a strong idea of your own, feel free to use that instead.

- Write a poem about a hero/heroine from recent times, for example Martin Luther King, Malala Yousafzai, Ranulph Fiennes, or Nelson Mandela
- Write the beginning of a folk story or fairy tale, told by you as a poem. It could be the original story, or your own modernised version, for example *Hansel and Gretel*, *The Three Little Pigs*, *Beauty and the Beast*.
- Write a rap about something that makes you angry, or something funny, or spooky, or unusual that has happened to you, a friend or a relative.
- Write a poem about a school event, lesson or playground scene.

■ Choose one of the options above. Remember to include some of the elements that you've learned about that make a poem memorable and enjoyable to listen to. You could write the whole poem and learn it off by heart, or just write down some words and phrases and improvise it, performing it freshly for the class.

■ Practise your poem and then perform it in front of your class.

■ When you have all performed your poems, discuss in groups what you were pleased with about your own performance and what you might do differently if you were to repeat the process.

The Choices Poets Make

THE CHOICES POETS MAKE

In this unit you are going to explore some of the choices poets make. Poems are intense, condensed texts and are often trying to express things which are difficult to put into words. They leave quite a lot for the reader to think about and use language in ways that could mean many different things. Poets make really careful decisions about what form the poem will take, its structure, layout, use of language and imagery, so that every single thing about the poem has been considered – what it says, how it says it, how it sounds, what it looks like on the page. Poets often draft and re-draft several times to get it right.

You will be exploring:

- ▶ The forms that poets choose
- ▶ The choices they make about imagery (metaphors, similes and so on)
- ▶ The choices they make about line breaks and layout
- ▶ The kind of voice they have.

THE CHOICES POETS MAKE

Choosing a Form 1 – Haiku

Poets can choose to write in many different forms, some very rule-governed, others more open and flexible. The most flexible choice is called 'free verse' because there are no fixed rules. Some contemporary poets write poems called 'prose poems' which are a blend of poetry and prose.

If a poet chooses a fixed form there are strict rules to follow. The haiku is one such form. It is a very old, traditional form but it has never lost its popularity. Many modern poets still write haiku.

What Is a Haiku?

The Japanese haiku is one of the most ancient forms and has been around since the 9th century. You may have come across haiku in primary school. The Japanese form has been adapted so that it works for the English language.

- On your own, read the translation of a haiku below, by Japanese master, Murakami Kijo (1865-1938), and think about your first response to it.

> First autumn morning:
> the mirror I stare into
> shows my father's face.

- As a class, discuss how far this haiku fulfils the criteria below.

The English form of a traditional haiku:

- Has only three lines – the first line has five syllables, the second has seven syllables, the third has five syllables
- Attempts to capture a particular moment in time
- Refers to nature, for example the seasons
- Uses simple language
- Presents an idea without telling the reader what to think
- Makes an unusual observation by comparing two subjects
- The two subjects are often separated by punctuation, such as a dash or a colon.

KS3 POETRY PLUS

James Berry's 'Haiku Moments 1'

Mixed-up haiku – making your own choices

Included on page 63 are the lines from three haiku by the poet James Berry, but they have been mixed up. They are part of a longer poem which includes six haiku in total. You are going to make choices of your own, drawing on what you know about the rules of haiku, to untangle them. You will need a photocopy of the mixed-up poems.

- Working with a partner, cut up the lines and rearrange them into three poems.

- With your partner, prepare an explanation for why you chose the arrangements you did. For example, what made you decide which were the last lines of each poem?

- Compare your versions with another pair. Do you agree?

- Compare your versions with those in the original on page 198. Notice that there are six haiku altogether. Look at the three new haiku and discuss similarities and differences between those and the ones you have been working on.

- Working with a partner, discuss how far you think James Berry's poem 'Haiku Moments 1' fulfils the description of traditional haiku that you read on page 61.

What haiku do

Many poets working with the haiku form have chosen to play around with the traditional form. For example, they have sometimes made changes to the number of syllables or lines or ignored the idea of comparing two subjects. If such changes are made, then what can we say about what makes a haiku? The American Academy of Poets uses this description:

> …a use of provocative, colourful images; an ability to be read in one breath; and a sense of sudden enlightenment and illumination.

- Working with a partner, discuss how far you think James Berry's poem fulfils the American Academy of Poets' description.

- As a class, discuss why you think he chose to write in the haiku form. Some possible reasons are given below to get your discussion started.

    ▶ Carrying on an ancient tradition

    ▶ A challenge

    ▶ Refreshing an ancient form for a modern audience.

THE CHOICES POETS MAKE

Mixed-up haiku

| Settled in the bowl |

| Stems and leaves downy |

| to be green sunlight. |

| alone, banana lies |

| Mango – you sucked from |

| there cuddle-curved, waiting. |

| this ripe scented flesh. |

| hidden here white under stone – |

| sunrise to sunset to be |

KS3 POETRY PLUS
Choosing a Form 2 – Freedom From Rules

Some poets choose to write in a form that follows a tight set of rules, but in this set of activities you are going to look at a poet who prefers a more free and easy approach. The poem you are going to read was first published in a book called *Lunch Poems*. The book was given this title both because the writer, Frank O'Hara, wrote poetry during his lunch break and because it was a pocket-sized book of short poems that a reader could enjoy on their own lunch break.

A Poem From the News

This poem was inspired by a newspaper article (reproduced on page 65), about Lana Turner, a film star who had a 50-year career which began in 1936 when she was just 16-years old.

- Listen and follow along while your teacher reads the newspaper report out loud.

- With a partner, predict how someone might turn this report into a poem. What length would it be? What form? What feelings or ideas might it try to put across?

- Now listen while your teacher reads the poem. (See page 197.)

- With your partner, share your first responses to the poem.

- In what ways has O'Hara drawn on, adapted and added to the details from the newspaper article?

Lana Turner Faints; in Hospital

Lana Turner is resting in Hollywood Presbyterian Hospital today after a collapse ascribed to 'nervous exhaustion'.

Miss Turner collapsed during a party in honor of her 42nd birthday at the end of a day's shooting at Paramount Studios. She had been working on a film entitled 'Who's Got the Action?'

The hospital said her condition was not considered serious. A spokesman for Miss Turner said she probably would return to work Monday. 'She's just exhausted,' her fifth husband, Fred May, said. 'She's been getting only four or five hours sleep a night.'

She was taken to the hospital by Eddie Albert, the actor and his wife, Margo, the actress. Also at the birthday party were actors Dean Martin, Paul Ford and Jack Rose, and director Daniel Mann.

KS3 POETRY PLUS
Getting Inside the Poet's Head

Frank O'Hara

Obviously we can't get inside the poet's head, but a role-play interview in which you take it in turns to play the poet can help you to consider some of the choices he made and why he made them.

The following questions are designed to help you think about the choices O'Hara might have made.

- Working with a partner, take it in turns to ask the questions to each other.

- When it is your turn, answer in role as the poet. If you find a question too hard to answer, discuss together what O'Hara might have said.

    - Why did you want to write this poem?
    - What do you want your readers to take away from this poem?
    - Does your poem have a serious message, or is it just a bit of fun?
    - Can you explain why there is more skill in writing a poem like this than might first appear?
    - Why have you only used punctuation twice, once in the title and once in the poem?
    - Is this a personal poem, or a poem about Lana Turner?
    - What are you trying to say about what poetry is, or what it should be?

THE CHOICES POETS MAKE

Over to You – Writing Like Frank O'Hara

O'Hara's poem captures a set of thoughts he had during one lunch break.

- On your own, or in pairs, try writing a poem of your own, for a collection that has one of the following titles:
    - On the Way Home
    - Mid-morning Break
    - Weekend
    - School Holiday

- Pick something very small – a moment or small experience that wouldn't necessarily seem very important to anyone else.
    - Try, like Frank O'Hara, to capture everything about that moment and your feelings, including random thoughts, other people's actions, what you noticed going on around you and so on.
    - Try, like O'Hara, to get across a strong sense of how you felt – happy, sad, confused, angry, puzzled, awkward or whatever emotion it was, even though your poem might seem like a collection of impressions.

Like O'Hara, try drafting your poem quickly to capture your spontaneous thoughts and feelings without worrying too much about making a poem. Afterwards, return to your draft and refine it, making careful choices to get your ideas across in an interesting way.

- Share your poems, either in small groups or as a whole class.

KS3 POETRY PLUS

Choosing a Form 3 – Pulling It All Together

Working in a group of four or five, you are going to put together a collection of poems which you think show poets making interesting choices of form. You can choose from the poems in the Anthology (pages 169-220) or from other poetry books that are available to you at school or in the library.

- Each person in your group should take responsibility for choosing three poems they would like to include. Be ready to justify your choices by explaining why the poems you have found are particularly good examples of poets making interesting choices of form.

- Share your poems and your reasons for wanting to include them.

- Narrow your group selection down to five or six really strong poems.

- Each person should take responsibility for writing a short introduction to one poem, explaining why it has been included in your collection.

- Choose a title for your collection, for example 'The Shape of Feelings'.

- If you have time, you could collate your selections into a class anthology. Where several groups have chosen the same poem, include all the different introductions.

Choosing an Image

Poets often use images. An image is when one thing stands for, or represents something else. So for instance, if you say, 'Life isn't a bed of roses', you don't literally mean that. You mean life isn't always easy.

- In small groups, look at the chart on page 69. It lists 10 images and what they represent. See if you can label each image using the correct terms, as listed below.

  ▶ When something is compared with something else using 'like' or 'as' it's called a **simile** (for example, love is like an ice cream sundae)

  ▶ When something is compared directly with something, as if it is the thing, it's called a **metaphor** (for example, death is a dark cloud)

  ▶ When something non-human (like the weather) is described in human terms, we say that the poet has used **personification** (for example, a storm described as an angry old man)

  ▶ When something associated with an idea is used to stand for it, it's called **metonymy** (for example, the crown standing for the monarchy).

THE CHOICES POETS MAKE

Poets try to find fresh images, rather than the obvious ones that we've all heard so often that we barely even realise they are images. Fresh images make the reader think, or feel, or understand things in new ways. They draw attention to themselves.

- Look again at the images in the chart. Decide which ones you think are old, stale ones and which ones are more interesting, unusual ones.

- Pick the one you find most interesting and prepare to give your reasons to the whole class.

Images	What it represents
It's bucketing down	RAIN
My heart is broken	LOVE
I felt cold as a pack of frozen peas	COLD
A yeasty, warm little ball of dough	A BABY
The very houses were asleep	A CITY AT NIGHT
Looking like a wet puppy on a muddy walk	LOOKING A MESS
Like a ballet dancer's frilly pink tutu	A WEDDING CAKE
My compass, showing me the way	A HUSBAND OR WIFE
Leaves falling from a tree	LOST FRIENDS
Fire and water and ice and earth and air	POETRY
The sun casts her motherly warmth over me	THE SUN
She earns her living by the pen	WRITING

KS3 POETRY PLUS

Choosing Images – A Poem About Autumn

Bearing in mind the earlier activity on fresh images, you are going to look at a poem by T.E. Hulme that uses imagery in interesting ways to write about autumn.

- As a class, read the poem, below.

> **Autumn**
>
> A touch of cold in the Autumn night—
> I walked abroad,
> And saw the ruddy moon lean over a hedge
> Like a red-faced farmer.
> I did not stop to speak, but nodded,
> And round about were the wistful stars
> With white faces like town children.
>
> T.E. Hulme

- As a class, discuss what you first notice about the poem. It may help you to know a few factual things:

  - In the early autumn the moon often appears low in the sky and is a reddish gold. It is called the 'harvest moon' as it appears around the time that farmers bring in their harvest.

  - 'I walked abroad' means 'I walked out into the countryside'.

  - At the time when Hulme wrote this poem, the phrase 'town children' would probably have conjured up the image of pale-skinned children who didn't get outdoors much and who, especially in the autumn and winter, lived in an atmosphere with lots of smog (a thick, dark fog caused by pollution from coal).

THE CHOICES POETS MAKE

Interviewing the Poet

- Working individually, create three or four questions to ask Hulme about the images he chose in his poem. For example, you could ask: When you described the moon 'leaning over the fence', what were you trying to put across?

- Join a partner. Take it in turns to interview the writer and to be the writer. When you are playing the writer, stay in role to answer the questions.

- As a class, feedback some of the more interesting questions and answers from your role play.

Over to You – Working With an Image

T.E. Hulme came up with lots of images and lines for poems. Some of them he later turned into full poems, some stayed as just a few lines. You are going to borrow one or two of Hulme's lines as the starting point for a poem of your own.

- Choose one of the fragments, below. (Fragment B describes the moon.)

- Brainstorm some ideas about how to use your fragment in a poem. You could use it as the opening and continue it, use the lines anywhere in your poem, or simply take an idea from the lines and use it as inspiration. For example, here's how one person started their poem, using fragment A:

My heart was scaffolding once.
Now it is an old house
casting long winter shadows.

Images by T.E. Hulme to use as starting points

A. Old houses were scaffolding once
   and workmen whistling.

B. What seemed so far away
   Is but a child's balloon, forgotten after play.

C. Oh, God, make small
   The old star-eaten blanket of the sky.

D. My mind is a corridor. The minds about me are corridors.

KS3 POETRY PLUS

Choosing Line Breaks and Layout

If poets aren't writing in a set form, like a haiku or a sonnet, they have much more flexibility about where they break lines, start a new stanza or use the space on the page to make a particular idea stand out on its own.

The activity that follows will help you see how much difference these decisions can make.

Song From the Kitlinuharmiut (Copper Eskimo)

Knud Rasmussen (1879-1933), shown above when on expedition, was a Greenlandic/Danish polar explorer and anthropologist. He heard the poem you are going to explore next when he was with a group of Kitlinuharmiut Inuit and was probably the first person to write it down.

The version you are going to hear is obviously not the original because it is in English. However, you are going to consider some of the decisions Rasmussen would have made when originally transcribing it. In particular you are going to think about:

- ▶ What exactly was said
- ▶ How to set out the poem.

■ Your teacher will read you the poem three times (page 194). Don't look at it yourself – just listen to the readings. You are going to work together in a group of three to try to re-create it as closely as you can in writing. This will involve you choosing how to set it out as a poem and where to put the line breaks.

THE CHOICES POETS MAKE

1. First reading

- Listen to your teacher reading the poem, without writing anything down. When your teacher has finished, jot down anything you remember. At this stage don't try to write out the whole poem.

- Join with your group to see what other people have noted down.

- Think about what to listen out for next.

2. Second reading

- Listen again and see what else you can add to your notes, individually.

- Join with your three – what have you got? Anything you are starting to notice? Add to your shared version.

- You have one more reading left, so plan how you are going to fill in the gaps between you.

3. Third reading and writing your poem

- Listen one more time. Again, share in your three and see how much of the poem you can put together. Discuss:
  - Where you will start a new line
  - Whether you will have more than one stanza
  - Where you will put in punctuation.
- Write out your final poem.

4. Reflection

- In your group, look at the published version on page 194 and compare this with your own. What do you notice about similarities and differences in the decisions you made about line breaks and layout?

- Is there anything you prefer in the published poem? Is there anything you prefer in your poem?

- Share your thoughts as a whole class.

KS3 POETRY PLUS
Choosing Words, Phrasing and Punctuation

You're going to look at two very different poems and decide which aspects of language choice seem to you to be most important and interesting and why.

- Work in small groups. Read the two poems on pages 75 and 76 out loud, one after the other.

- In your group, talk about your first thoughts and impressions. What are they like? What do they seem to be about? Which one do you like best and why?

- Still in your group, look at the list below of the choices poets make in their uses of language. For each one, decide which of the two poems it applies to more, and talk about why you made that decision. For each one, also talk about the effect of that choice.

- For each poem, pick the one choice the poet has made that you think is most interesting. Prepare to explain this to the rest of the class, giving your reasons and suggesting what you think the impact of that choice is on the ideas and feelings expressed in the poem.

> **Some choices of words, phrasing and punctuation**
> - Unusual punctuation
> - Sentences that end at the end of a stanza
> - Sentences that are simple and easy to read aloud
> - Sentences that are long, complicated and sometimes unfinished
> - Odd ways of ending lines and starting new ones
> - Words that are monosyllabic (only one syllable, for example 'wet' rather than 'saturated')
> - Everyday words – the kind of thing you might find in many different kinds of texts
> - Poetic or literary words – the kind of words you'd mainly find in literature
> - Repetition of the same words or phrases
> - Using repeated lines in a playful way
> - Very few adjectives or adverbs, describing things and actions
> - Full of rich words to add detail to things and actions
> - Words where the sounds suggest something important, for example echoing the meaning
> - Rhyme used to emphasise words, or give a satisfying sense of things being complete.

632

The Brain—is wider than the Sky—
For—put them side by side—
The one the other will contain
With ease—and You—beside—

The Brain is deeper than the sea—
For—hold them—Blue to Blue—
The one the other will absorb—
As Sponges—Buckets—do—

The Brain is just the weight of God—
For—Heft them—Pound for Pound—
And they will differ—if they do—
As Syllable from Sound—

Emily Dickinson

Poem #907 Miss Charlotte Brown, Librarian, Goes Mad

Today, I have decided
to read every poem ever written
in the short history of our civilization.
I know it is a selfish thing

to read. Every poem ever written
has its good intentions. I know,
I know, it is a selfish thing.
I want to believe that. Poetry

has its good intentions. I know
reading poems can't help much.
I want to believe that poetry
books have the answer. I'll start

reading. Poems can't help much
in the short history of our civilization.
Books have the answer. I'll start
today. I have decided.

Felix Jung

THE CHOICES POETS MAKE

Choosing a Voice

Voice in poetry is quite a tricky idea. One aspect of voice is the idea of a poet finding their own unique 'voice' – in other words something recognisable about the way their poems speak to readers. It's a bit like our speaking voices. No two people have the same voice. Each person's voice is unique and recognisable, even if you only hear a tiny snatch of them speaking.

Another aspect is the idea of taking on different voices. For example, it's worth being aware that just because a poet uses 'I', it doesn't mean to say that it's them speaking as themselves. It might be that they are using a narrator, or creating a separate 'persona' – an 'I' who speaks but who isn't the poet.

> When you talk about voice in a poem, these are the kinds of things you might talk about:
> - Whose voice speaks to you
> - Whether the voice of the poet is intimate and personal or distant and impersonal
> - A voice that is distinctive, individual, quirky, original and so on
> - Whether the voice seems to belong to a persona (a character in the poem)
> - The tone of voice. A list of some of the tones of voice you might find in a poem are listed here.
>
> | | | | |
> |---|---|---|---|
> | Aggressive | Cheerful | Hopeful | Questioning |
> | Angry | Confrontational | Jokey | Quiet |
> | Argumentative | Determined | Light-hearted | Reflective |
> | Bitter | Direct | Matter-of-fact | Resigned |
> | Bold | Excited | Neutral | Sad |
> | Celebratory | Fanciful | Passionate | Sarcastic |
> | Challenging | Grim | Puzzled | Satirical |

- Individually, choose any poem that you've looked at in the work you've done on poetry so far.

- Re-read the poem, thinking particularly about its voice and how you would describe it. Use the list above to help you, but try to go beyond just labelling it, to explain exactly what the voice is like and why.

- Get into small groups, making sure that each student has chosen a different poem. Share your poems and explain to each other what's special about the voice in each one.

KS3 POETRY PLUS
Reflection – Making Your Own Choice

- Choose a poem from *KS3 Poetry Plus* or elsewhere and imagine you are the poet who wrote it. Write three or four paragraphs in role as the poet about the choices you made in your writing. You should think about:

    ▶ Form

    ▶ Language

    ▶ Images

    ▶ Line breaks

    ▶ Voice

    ▶ Anything else that is interesting.

LOST IN TRANSLATION

molestum est teque non
rogāmus pauca verba Māternō
. in aurem sīc ut audiat sōl us.
ille trīstium lacernārum
baeticātus at— —phaeātus,
coccinā— —ōs e s s e.
am ethysti— —cat
la— —mper
fuscōs c— —mōrē s.
rogābit u— —ollem.
lavāmu— —ursum.
spectat oculis devorantibus
mentulās videt labrīs.

LOST IN TRANSLATION

KS3 POETRY PLUS

LOST IN TRANSLATION

> In this unit you are going to find out more about how poetry works by looking at what happens when someone tries to translate a poem into another language.
>
> You will consider how poetry works in different languages, have a go at doing some translation yourself, and think about whether all writing is, in a way, an act of translation.
>
> You will also write some bilingual or multilingual poetry along the way and get a chance to use any languages that you know other than English.

Your Experience of Translation

You will all have done some translating from one language into another. After all, you are all required to study a foreign language in school. So you will have translated between English and French or English and Spanish, for example.

Some of you will have a much broader experience of translation, perhaps because you speak more than one language fluently, or because you have travelled abroad.

■ In small groups, discuss the following and then feedback the main points of the discussion to the whole class.

- ▶ What other languages do you speak and write? You should include any languages you are learning or have learned at school, as well as ones you might speak at home.
- ▶ What is it like to speak and/or write in another language?
- ▶ When you speak or write in another language, do you find yourself translating from English into that language, or is the language simply there in your head?
- ▶ How do other languages sound in your mouth, or look on the page, compared to English?
- ▶ Do you ever speak or write using more than one language at the same time? Or have you heard anyone else doing this? If so, what is it like?
- ▶ Do you ever use Google Translate, or other translation programmes? If so, what is your experience of them?

LOST IN TRANSLATION

Translating Poetry – The Challenges

Translating from one language to another is not simply a question of replacing a word from one language with a different word from another. A word or phrase from one language might not have quite the same meaning or connotations in another. And some words or phrases simply do not exist in other languages. The problem is particularly acute in poetry, where the original choice of words and their placement is done with such care.

Some of the challenges faced when translating poetry are listed below.

- As a class, discuss the nature of each challenge, thinking about why it might raise problems for a translator. Can you think of any possible solutions to these challenges?

> ### The challenges
>
> It's hard to…
>
> - Translate words and maintain the sound and rhythm of a poem
> - Translate words where there isn't an equivalent in the other language, for example there is no French equivalent for 'cool' when it refers to something impressive; the Yiddish word ' chutzpah', which has connotations of extreme self-confidence or boldness, has no exact equivalent in English
> - Translate and keep the shape of a poem
> - Translate words that rhyme from one language into another
> - Translate to keep the word order of the original poem
> - Translate idioms from one language to another. An **idiom** is an expression that means something quite different from the actual words said, for example 'kicked the bucket' for 'died' or 'raining cats and dogs' for 'raining heavily'.

KS3 POETRY PLUS
Partial Translations

An interesting activity to draw attention to the original language of a poem, and to start thinking about translation, is to translate only a small number of words in a poem. The example below changes five words or phrases from a poem by Emily Brontë. This was done by cutting and pasting the original poem into Google Translate, setting the translation to French, then identifying words and phrases to draw on.

- In a pair, read the two poems out loud and identify the changes. (Don't worry too much about your pronunciation but some help is given, below.)

- Try to come up with one or two things you can say about the original poem that you have noticed by reading both versions side by side.

- Try to come up with one or two things you can say about how the changes alter the effect of the poem.

- Decide which you prefer, and feedback to your class with reasons.

Fall, leaves, fall	Fall, feuilles, fall
Fall, leaves, fall; die, flowers, away; Lengthen night and shorten day; Every leaf speaks bliss to me Fluttering from the autumn tree. I shall smile when wreaths of snow Blossom where the rose should grow; I shall sing when night's decay Ushers in a drearier day. *Emily Brontë*	Fall, feuilles, fall; die, flowers, away; Lengthen night and shorten day; Every feuille speaks bliss to me Fluttering from the autumn tree. Je vais sourire when wreaths of snow Blossom where the rose should grow; Je vais chanter when night's decay Ouvre la porte to drearier day.

Pronunciations
Feuilles: fur-yi
Vais: vay
Sourire: soo-rear
Ouvre: oov-re

LOST IN TRANSLATION

Writing Your Own Partial Translation

You are now going to write a partial translation of a poem yourselves. Unless you are fluent in more than one language, you will need access to Google Translate for this activity.

- Staying in your pair, identify a short poem you want to translate. This can be a poem from the Anthology (pages 169-220), or a favourite of your own. You might even use a poem that one of you has written.

- Write the English poem into Google Translate as shown below. Ideally you will have a poem that you can cut and paste from a Word file or the Internet.

- Identify a language you want to translate the poem into and select it on the right-hand box of Google Translate. Unless you are familiar with another alphabetic script, make sure you select a language that uses the same alphabet as English.

- Read both versions side by side and experiment with replacing some of the English words with ones from the other language.

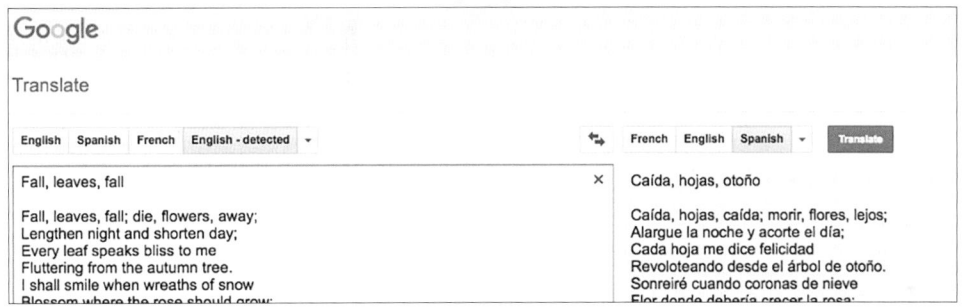

Google Translate

English | Spanish | French | English - detected

Fall, leaves, fall
Fall, leaves, fall; die, flowers, away;
Lengthen night and shorten day;
Every leaf speaks bliss to me
Fluttering from the autumn tree.
I shall smile when wreaths of snow
Blossom where the rose should grow.

French | English | Spanish | Translate

Caída, hojas, otoño
Caída, hojas, caída; morir, flores, lejos;
Alargue la noche y acorte el día;
Cada hoja me dice felicidad
Revoloteando desde el árbol de otoño.
Sonreiré cuando coronas de nieve
Flor donde debería crecer la rosa;

- Cut and paste your final translation into a Word document next to the original.

- Write a short explanation of why you chose particular words and phrases in translation, and the effect they have on the poem. Here is an example of the kind of things you might say, looking at the English – French translation of 'Fall, leaves, Fall' from the previous activity.

> The choice of 'feuilles' instead of leaves adds to the alliterative effect of the poem, linking it strongly to 'fall' and 'flowers' in the first line, and later 'fluttering'. The phrases 'je vais sourire' and 'je vais chanter' are similarly patterned to the English 'I shall smile' and 'I shall sing'. However, I think 'je vais sourire' is more rhythmic and 'je vais chanter' (pronounced 'shontay') creates an internal rhyme in that line with 'decay'. 'Ouvre la porte' on the final line literally mean 'opens the door', which I feel is a more poetic phrase than 'usher in'.
>
> I decided not to change the words at the end of a line because this would disrupt the rhyme scheme.

- Listen to a range of partial translations round the class, along with explanations of changes made.

KS3 POETRY PLUS
Reading Different Translations

Below is a French poem. Two English translations of it are included on page 85.

- In pairs, read the French poem out loud. Do not look at the English versions at this point, even if you don't know any French. Try to come up with two interesting things you can say about this poem even if you don't understand it!

- Next read the two different translations of the French poem and discuss the following with your partner:
  - What are the differences between the two translations?
  - Do the differences change the meaning or effect of the poem?
  - Which do you prefer and why?

- Try to write your own version of the poem that improves on the two translations. You can borrow from both, change words and word order, and so on.

- Listen to a selection of your new translations round the class.

- Finally, discuss as a whole class the following question:

> When translating a poem, is it more important to stick as closely as possible to the original language and form, or to write a good poem, even if the meaning of the original changes?

Les Roses de Saadi

J'ai voulu ce matin te rapporter des roses;
Mais j'en avais tant pris dans mes ceintures closes
Que les noeuds trop serrés n'ont pu les contenir.

Les noeuds ont éclaté. Les roses envolées
Dans le vent, à la mer s'en sont toutes allées.
Elles ont suivi l'eau pour ne plus revenir;

La vague en a paru rouge et comme enflammée.
Ce soir, ma robe encore en est toute embaumée…
Respires-en sur moi l'odorant souvenir.

Marceline Desbordes-Valmore

LOST IN TRANSLATION

Translation 1

(This version tries to translate the language word for word as closely as possible)

> I wanted this morning to bring you roses
> But I had taken so many in my closed belts
> That the knots which were too tight could not contain them.
> The knots broke. The roses flew away
> In the wind, they all went to the sea.
> They followed the water never to return.
> The wave appeared red and as if inflamed.
> Tonight my dress is still completely embalmed…
> Breathe on me the fragrant memory.

Translation 2

(This version tries to use the same rhyme scheme and rhythm as closely as possible)

> I wanted this morning to bring you roses
> But they were packed so tight within my hosiers
> That they could not be contained.
> Released, they were set in motion
> Carried by wind and over ocean,
> Lost to water, unretained.
> The waves turned red, carrying fire.
> At night my clothes still hold scent of desire…
> Breathe on me sweet scent.

Marceline Desbordes-Valmore

KS3 POETRY PLUS

Lipograms – Translating From English Into English!

A lipogram is a form of writing that deliberately avoids using a particular letter. Believe it or not a French writer called Georges Perec wrote an entire novel, *La Disparation*, without using the letter 'e'. Even more amazingly a writer called Gilbert Adair translated it into English, giving it the title *A Void*. The translation was 50 pages longer than the original!

You are now going to write a lipogram in order to 'translate' a poem into English. This task will help you to reflect on the choices available when translating, some of the challenges faced, and solutions for overcoming them.

- In pairs, 'translate' 'The Eagle', by Alfred, Lord Tennyson (below) into a poem that does not use the letter 'e'. The title of the poem is included in the task. This is very difficult to do, so feel free to be as imaginative and innovative as you like. It would be helpful to have access to a thesaurus, or to use the synonym function on a computer – try to get started without using either of these, though.

- Join up with other pairs and compare your translations.

- Discuss as a whole class the different ways that you translated the poem, the difficulties you faced, and what the process showed you about translation, language and meaning.

> **The Eagle**
>
> He clasps the crag with crooked hands;
> Close to the sun in lonely lands,
> Ring'd with the azure world, he stands.
>
> The wrinkled sea beneath him crawls;
> He watches from his mountain walls,
> And like a thunderbolt he falls.

Azure = bright blue

LOST IN TRANSLATION

Combining Two Versions of a Poem

A student was asked to write a poem about an oxbow lake for Geography homework. Frustrated by their initial efforts, they decided to see what would happen if they cut and pasted what they had written into Google Translate and then translated back and forth between different languages. They went from English to Spanish to Indonesian to Albanian to Persian to Esperanto and back to English again.

The results were surprising. As the student expected, the final translated version was very different from the original. But they actually preferred some of the words and phrases in the new version!

- Working in a pair, read both poems on pages 88-89 and discuss:
    - The poetic qualities of each
    - What could be done to improve them both
    - What the English translation programme might have found tricky about the original.

- Now work on your own to write a poem about an oxbow lake that you think combines the best elements of both poems. You can add in ideas of your own, but need to largely rely on these two versions. You might like to think about:
    - Rhyme
    - Rhythm and sound
    - Imagery
    - Word choice and word order
    - Meaning – do you want it to be obvious or less obvious?

- Finally, in pairs, talk about your poem and the choices you made. Make sure you consider what makes your poem a good one, and how you want readers to respond.

KS3 POETRY PLUS

The Oxbow Lake

(Student's original version)

> The Oxbow Lake
> Once this was a relaxed river
> Meandering through the landscape
> With no urgency to deliver
> A yawn's sense of direction
> Now with no time to pause
> It flows straight
> Life has purpose, life has cause
> A devotee to energy and current
> The old river is sealed off
> Imprisoned in an oxbow bend
> A redundant, lifeless trough
> A billabong.

Billabong = an aboriginal word for an oxbow lake

The Oxbow Lake

(Google Translate version)

> Lake Albion
> It was a quiet flow
> The coast through the landscape
> There is no urgent transfer
> The sense of the road disappeared
> Now it's not time to stop
> Custom flow
> Life is an object, life is the goal
> Interested in energy and current
> The old river was severely closed
> Prisoner on the neck curve
> Additional and immovable channels
> Bilobang

Bilobang = a native word for the bushes of the lake

KS3 POETRY PLUS

Using Your Home Language

This activity is for those of you who are comfortable speaking and writing languages other than English.

- First, complete one of the following writing activities:
  - ▶ Translate a poem that you like that is written in English into another language.
  - ▶ Write a 'multilingual' poem that combines English with your other language or languages.
  - ▶ Write a poem in a language other than English. Translate this into English.

- Whichever activity you chose, write a few paragraphs about the experience of writing it. You might like to think about:
  - ▶ What it feels like to use other languages in an English lesson.
  - ▶ How confident you are using a language other than English.
  - ▶ How the effect of your poetry changes when you use different languages.

- If you are pleased with your poem, you might want to read it aloud (with its translation) for other members of the class to hear.

Pulling It All Together

Look back over everything you have done during this unit and do the following things:

- Choose the poem you most enjoyed working on and write a short paragraph explaining why.

- Choose which of these statements you think best express what you have learnt about poetry by doing the translations and explain why.

A.	Every word matters, not just because of what it says but because it is part of a pattern of words that work together.
B.	Sound is just as important as sense in poetry.
C.	The way words look on the page makes a big difference to how you read a poem.
D.	Poetry is almost impossible to translate – it's not just about using a dictionary and substituting words.
E.	What goes into a poem is much more complicated than I realised before.

STUDY OF A POET: ROBERT FROST

KS3 POETRY PLUS

STUDY OF A POET – ROBERT FROST

In this section you will have a chance to think about what makes a poet unique by studying several poems by the same poet.

Robert Frost (1874-1963) is one of the most well-known and best-loved American poets. In his lifetime, he received many awards for his poetry.

He is particularly known for poems which use everyday language and seem simple on the surface, but which have deeper underlying themes. Expect to read simple words that make you think hard!

Acquainted With the Night

Questioning a Poem

In this activity you are going to read Robert Frost's 'Acquainted with the Night' three times, exploring some questions about the poem. Over your three readings you will get a flavour of Frost's poetry and notice how your ideas about it change and develop. You may photocopy the poem on page 93.

First reading

- Listen as your teacher reads the poem 'Acquainted with the Night' aloud.

- Working on your own, annotate the poem with as many questions as you can. Questions that ask 'why', for example 'Why is he walking in the rain?' or 'Why does the poet repeat X?', might be particularly interesting to try to answer, so make sure you include some of those.

- Share some of your questions as a class.

- Make a note of any questions you would now like to add to your own.

STUDY OF A POET: ROBERT FROST

Acquainted With the Night

I have been one acquainted with the night.
I have walked out in rain—and back in rain.
I have outwalked the furthest city light.

I have looked down the saddest city lane.
I have passed by the watchman on his beat
And dropped my eyes, unwilling to explain.

I have stood still and stopped the sound of feet
When far away an interrupted cry
Came over houses from another street,

But not to call me back or say good-by;
And further still at an unearthly height
One luminary clock against the sky

Proclaimed the time was neither wrong nor right.
I have been one acquainted with the night.

Robert Frost

KS3 POETRY PLUS

Second reading

- Read the poem again, to yourself.

- Look through your questions:
    - Cross out any that now seem unimportant
    - Choose one question you think will be useful and interesting to explore further.

Third reading

- Working in a group of three, read the poem again together.

- Take it in turns to share the question that you thought would be interesting or useful to explore.

- Try to answer each other's questions and use them as the basis for a discussion about the poem.

Evaluating Readings of 'Acquainted With the Night'

Your three readings will have given you an understanding of the poem which you are going to develop further in this activity. A Diamond Nine diagram is a way of organising ideas to show their importance. The diagram below shows you how to do this. The most important ideas are placed towards the top and the least important towards the bottom. Ideas of roughly equal importance are placed in the same row.

- Working in a three, read the statements about the poem on page 95 and discuss how to pick nine and put them into a Diamond 9 shape.

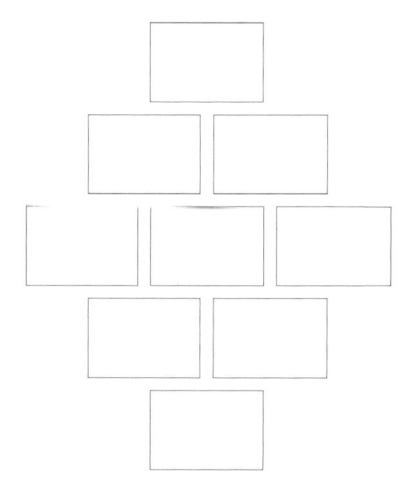

- As a class, share some of the ideas from your discussion.

STUDY OF A POET: ROBERT FROST

Statements on 'Acquainted With the Night'

A. At first this seems like a fairly simple poem about someone going for a walk at night.

B. This poem creates a sense of aimless sadness.

C. Seven lines in the poem begin 'I have…', perhaps making us think of the trudging steps of the narrator on his dreary walk.

D. This is not a walk the speaker is taking for pleasure.

E. The use of repetition gives the reader a sense that the narrator can see no escape, from the walking, from his thoughts and feelings, even from the rain.

F. Several lines in the poem suggest that the speaker sees himself as separate from everyone else, for example he mentions someone crying out, but that it was not for him.

G. The phrase 'acquainted with the night' suggests that the speaker has got to know the night only too well, because he does this walk often.

H. The first line is repeated as the last line, giving the sense of walking in circles, of there being no way out.

I. The night-time setting and the rain emphasise the speaker's lack of connection with other people in the city who are sensibly at home and asleep.

J. This poem isn't really about walking at night. The night walk is a poetic way of representing feelings of isolation and sadness.

K. Darkness and light are contrasted in the poem, suggesting something about the speaker's feelings.

L. 'I have' suggests that the experiences described aren't necessarily over.

KS3 POETRY PLUS

Developing Your Critical Writing

- Working individually, use the statements from the Diamond 9 activity to help you to write one or more paragraphs about the poem. You can:
  - Include as many or as few of the statements as you like
  - Change the wording of the statements as much as you like to express your own views and so that your paragraph reads well
  - Use the statements in any order.
- Share some of your work around the class and discuss the questions, below.
  - Were there any particularly popular statements, or any that were not used by anyone? Why/why not?
  - If a statement says something like 'This poem creates a sense of aimless sadness', what else do you need to do to turn this into good critical writing?
  - Which paragraphs work particularly well? What do you notice about them?

STUDY OF A POET: ROBERT FROST

The Road Not Taken

The poem you are going to explore next is probably Robert Frost's most famous. It offers real insight into how his poetry can look very simple on the surface, while conveying deep messages underneath.

The Road Less Travelled

You may have come across a famous quotation from the poem you are going to read: 'The one less travelled', although it is usually quoted as 'the road less travelled'. 'The road less travelled' is the title of eight different music albums. It has been used in a voiceover for an advert about a man making a good choice about which car to buy. It is the name of a travel company. It has been taken as the title of several books such as:

> *The Road Less Travelled* by Bill Bryson
> **Here is an extract from the blurb on the book cover.**
>
> 'Avoid crowded tourist hotspots and discover the lesser-known wonders of the world with this beautifully illustrated guide to off-the-beaten-track sights, experiences and destinations.'

> *The Road Less Travelled* by Morgan Scott Peck
> **Here is an extract from the blurb on the book cover.**
>
> 'A self-help book about embracing rather than avoiding life's difficulties.'

- As a class, discuss what the phrase 'the road less travelled' might mean and why the quotation has become so popular.

KS3 POETRY PLUS

A Metaphor For Life

A path, road or journey of some kind is a commonly used metaphor (or simile) for life.

- On your own, draw a quick sketch representing your life as a path, road or journey of some kind. Think about how you will represent important moments. For example, a crossroads might represent an important choice.

- As a class, talk about how you represented some different aspects of your life (you don't need to share specific, personal details) and why a path, journey or road is such a commonly used metaphor for life.

True or False?

- Now listen and follow along as your teacher reads the poem on page 100.

- With a partner, read the poem again more slowly and carefully and discuss whether the statements below are true or false. They are designed to help you think carefully about what exactly the poem has to say on a literal, or surface level.

- Share your ideas as a class and try to resolve any differences of opinion by referring back to what is said in the poem.

A.	One road is more attractive to the traveller than the other.

B.	The traveller could see that one road was less used than the other because it was less worn down.

C.	The traveller will come back another day to try the other path.

D.	At some point in the distant future, the traveller will tell the story of his decision about which road to take.

E.	The traveller took the road that fewer people had travelled down.

STUDY OF A POET: ROBERT FROST

Looking Beneath the Surface – Your View and Your Response

The poem clearly has a meaning beneath the surface – the road referred to stands for something else; presumably it is a metaphor for a journey through life.

Following on from this metaphor, many readers think that the poem is suggesting that you should make your own way in life rather than just following everyone else. However, some people, including some poetry experts, disagree with this.

- Working individually, decide which statement or statements, below, sum up your own opinion about the metaphorical meaning of the poem. Be ready to explain your reasons.

- Share your decisions and reasons as a class.

- Now, working on your own again, decide which statement you most agree with. Write a few sentences justifying your decision, referring to the poem as you do so.

> A. This is a poem about how important it is to make the right choices in life.

> B. This is a poem about making your own way instead of following the crowd.

> C. This is a poem about the fact that whatever choice you take, you just have to make the best of it.

> D. This is a poem about wanting to go back in time and change your mind about a difficult decision.

> E. This is a poem about the fact that you can never know whether you made the right decision because you can't go back and change it.

The Road Not Taken

Two roads diverged in a yellow wood,
And sorry I could not travel both
And be one traveler, long I stood
And looked down one as far as I could
To where it bent in the undergrowth;

Then took the other, as just as fair,
And having perhaps the better claim,
Because it was grassy and wanted wear;
Though as for that, the passing there
Had worn them really about the same,

And both that morning equally lay
In leaves no step had trodden black.
Oh, I kept the first for another day!
Yet knowing how way leads on to way,
I doubted if I should ever come back.

I shall be telling this with a sigh
Somewhere ages and ages hence:
Two roads diverged in a wood, and I—
I took the one less traveled by,
And that has made all the difference.

Robert Frost

STUDY OF A POET: ROBERT FROST

Over to You – An Extended Metaphor

▎ You are going to write your own poem based around an extended metaphor. Use the 'random metaphor generator' below to help you to choose a topic for your poem and a metaphor to use as a comparison.

▎ Brainstorm some ways in which you could use your metaphor. An example has been done for you to show you what kind of thing you could do.

▎ Turn your ideas into a short poem with an extended metaphor.

Random metaphor generator

Topics	Metaphors
Passing an exam	A flower
A misunderstanding with a friend	Road signs
Adopting a bold new look	Bungee jumping
Being grounded by your parents	A skateboard
A break up	A baby learning to walk
Getting into trouble for something you didn't do	A storm
Winning an award	A fruit salad
Learning something new	Falling into a river
A difficult conversation	A knot
Having a crush on someone	A spider's web

A break up is like a skateboard because

- you feel free
- a leap into the unknown
- it looks easier when someone else is doing it
- there are no rules
- everyone does it differently
- it's hard to steer
- practice makes perfect
- you get hurt
- the wheels came off

101

© ENGLISH & MEDIA CENTRE, 2018

KS3 POETRY PLUS
Nothing Gold Can Stay

Making Predictions

As you've probably already noticed, Robert Frost often uses a simple story or description of something concrete to express something more abstract and hard to explain – thoughts or feelings or a theme. For example, the night time walk in 'Acquainted with the Night', was a way of talking about the theme of isolation and sadness; and the road in 'The Road not Taken' was an extended metaphor for life and life decisions.

You are going to read another poem by Frost called 'Nothing Gold Can Stay' on page 104, exploring it as a whole class.

- Before reading the poem, talk about the title and discuss what the theme of the poem might be. What abstract ideas might Frost be about to explore with such a title?

- Discuss any other ideas about what this poem might be like before you read it, based on what you already know about Frost's poems. For example, what will it look like on the page? How long will it be? Will it use an extended metaphor and, if so, in what way? What kind of language might it use? Will it use rhythm and rhyme?

- Note down all your ideas on the board, before going on to read 'Nothing Gold Can Stay'. Your teacher will explain to you any words or references you don't know, like 'hue' or 'Eden', before you work on the poem further.

Matching Predictions With Reality

- As a class, read 'Nothing Gold Can Stay' again and talk about the following:
  - Is the poem as you expected? Consider the theme, layout, length, use of extended metaphor, language, rhythm, rhyme and so on.
  - In what ways is the poem different from what you expected?
  - What do you think the poem is about?

- As a class, write one or two sentences that sum up for you the most important things about the poem. Try to include not only what it seems to be about but also how it says it. Be prepared to add, adapt and edit till you get one or two sentences that express your agreed ideas really well.

STUDY OF A POET: ROBERT FROST

Over to You – Writing Your Own Version

Poet Sophie Hannah wrote her own light-hearted version of 'Nothing Gold Can Stay'. You can read it on page 104.

▌ Look at these two views and decide which you agree with most:

> **View 1:**
> Hannah's poem is a bit of silly fun, with no serious theme or message.

> **View 2:**
> Hannah is saying just the same important things as Frost, about time passing.

▌ Working individually, you are going to write your own poem based on 'Nothing Gold Can Stay'. Your poem can be serious or witty, use modern or poetic language.

Your poem must have:

- ▶ 8 lines
- ▶ An aa, bb, cc, dd rhyme scheme
- ▶ A simple subject which explores a similar theme (such as death, loss, the way that nothing lasts for ever and so on). Come up with your own idea, or use one of the suggestions, below.
  - – Phones become obsolete very quickly
  - – Birthday candles burn
  - – Children all grow up
  - – Biscuits turn to crumbs
  - – Holidays always end.

KS3 POETRY PLUS

Robert Frost's poem

Nothing Gold Can Stay

Nature's first green is gold,
Her hardest hue to hold.
Her early leaf's a flower;
But only so an hour.
Then leaf subsides to leaf.
So Eden sank to grief,
So dawn goes down to day.
Nothing gold can stay.

Robert Frost

Sophie Hannah's poem

Trainers All Turn Grey

(after Robert Frost's 'Nothing Gold Can Stay)

You buy your trainers new.
They cost a bob or two.
At first they're clean and white,
The laces thick and tight.
Then they must touch the ground –
(You have to walk around).
You learn to your dismay
Trainers all turn grey.

Sophie Hannah

STUDY OF A POET: ROBERT FROST

Author Study – Pulling It All Together

- As a class, think about the Frost poems you have looked at and discuss some of the similarities and differences between them, using the prompts below to help you.

- Choose four or five of the bullet points and write about the role each plays in Frost's poetry.

> **Which poems…**
> - Are about something literal, but also have a deeper meaning
> - Use an extended metaphor to explore an abstract idea
> - Refer to nature
> - Use everyday language
> - Seem simple at first, but make a serious point
> - Use humour
> - Have a regular rhyme scheme
> - Have a regular rhythm
> - Have several stanzas of the same length
> - Have a title that is simple, using words from the poem
> - Have a personal voice and seem to talk about personal experience?

KS3 POETRY PLUS

Author Study – Applying What You Know

- Working in pairs or threes, read the titles and lines below, taken from five poems.
  - Three of them are by Robert Frost
  - One is by a poet called Elizabeth Barrett Browning
  - One is by a poet called Geoffrey Hill.

- Drawing on what you have learned about Robert Frost's poetry, discuss which two you think are not by Frost and why.

- Share your ideas as a class, before your teacher gives you the answer.

1	**A Dust of Snow** The way a crow Shook down on me

2	**Meeting and Passing** As I went down the hill along the wall There was a gate I had leaned at for the view

3	**If thou must love me, let it be for nought** If thou must love me, let it be for nought Except for love's sake only. Do not say

4	**Putting in the Seed** You come to fetch me from my work to-night When supper's on the table, and we'll see

5	**An Apology for the Revival of Church Architecture in England** The pigeon purrs in the wood: the wood has gone; Dark leaves that flick to silver in the gust, And the marsh-orchids and the heron's nest, Goldgrimy shafts and pillars of the sun.

POETS SPEAKING OUT

KS3 POETRY PLUS
POETS SPEAKING OUT

> Poems can be about big, political issues and how they affect society, or about personal issues and how they affect an individual, or both.
>
> In this section you are going to look at poets expressing strong opinions about big issues, sometimes in quite a personal way. First you will focus on one poem in close detail to establish some initial ideas. Then you will use what you have learned to range across several poems in a more independent way. You will have the chance to write a poem of your own and to do some extended critical writing.

A Close Focus on a Single Poem

'Still I Rise', by Maya Angelou

As you work on Maya Angelou's poem 'Still I Rise', keep written notes to keep track of how your understanding develops.

Developing a reading

- Either listen to Maya Angelou reading 'Still I Rise' on YouTube or listen as your teacher reads the poem. If you listen on YouTube, be aware that Maya Angelou performed this poem many times over the years and sometimes made changes to the version on pages 110-111.

- Working on your own, read the poem on pages 110-111. Use some of the prompts on page 109 to help you to make written notes, recording your thoughts about the poem. (Choose whichever prompts help you to think about the poem and express your ideas about it. Don't just work through them as a list, saying very little about each one.)

- Work in a group of three or four. Use the same prompts (page 109) to have a discussion about the poem.

Tone of voice

- As a class, discuss which of the different tones of voice listed on page 109 you might expect people to use when speaking out on an issue they feel strongly about and which you would not expect them to use.

- Which tone, or tones of voice, do you think Maya Angelou uses in 'Still I Rise'? Does it change, or is it consistent throughout the poem? Do any lines in particular contribute to that tone?

POETS SPEAKING OUT

Prompts to help you develop a reading

- I like the way it…
- It reminds me of…
- I've noticed how it…
- … makes me think that the poem is written in a… tone of voice
- I'm puzzled by…
- It's interesting how…
- My favourite bit is…
- I'd like to know…
- It seems to be about…
- I think… but I'm not sure about…
- This poem makes me feel…

Possible tones of voice

- Aggressive
- Angry
- Argumentative
- Bitter
- Bold
- Celebratory
- Challenging
- Cheerful
- Confrontational
- Determined
- Direct
- Excited
- Grim
- Hopeful
- Jokey
- Light-hearted
- Matter-of-fact
- Neutral
- Passionate
- Puzzled
- Questioning
- Quiet
- Reflective
- Resigned
- Sad
- Sarcastic
- Satirical

Still I Rise

You may write me down in history
With your bitter, twisted lies,
You may trod me in the very dirt
But still, like dust, I'll rise.

Does my sassiness upset you?
Why are you beset with gloom?
'Cause I walk like I've got oil wells
Pumping in my living room.

Just like moons and like suns,
With the certainty of tides,
Just like hopes springing high,
Still I'll rise.

Did you want to see me broken?
Bowed head and lowered eyes?
Shoulders falling down like teardrops.
Weakened by my soulful cries?

Maya Angelou

POETS SPEAKING OUT

Does my haughtiness offend you?
Don't you take it awful hard
'Cause I laugh like I've got gold mines
Diggin' in my own backyard.

You may shoot me with your words,
You may cut me with your eyes,
You may kill me with your hatefulness,
But still, like air, I'll rise.

Does my sexiness upset you?
Does it come as a surprise
That I dance like I've got diamonds
At the meeting of my thighs?

Out of the huts of history's shame
I rise
Up from a past that's rooted in pain
I rise
I'm a black ocean, leaping and wide,
Welling and swelling I bear in the tide.

Leaving behind nights of terror and fear
I rise
Into a daybreak that's wondrously clear
I rise
Bringing the gifts that my ancestors gave,
I am the dream and the hope of the slave.
I rise
I rise
I rise.

Maya Angelou

KS3 POETRY PLUS

The Poem in Numbers

- Working in pairs, re-read the poem and complete a chart like the one below.
- Discuss with your partner what you find interesting about the number of times particular features are used.
- Share your findings and thoughts as a class.

Feature	Number of times used	Why might Angelou have made this choice?
Repetition of the phrase 'I rise' throughout the poem		
Rhetorical question		
Line ending with an 'ise' sound		
Four line stanza with the rhyme scheme A, B, C, B		
15 line stanza with an irregular structure		
Rhyming couplet		
Imagery connected to wealth and money		
Lines referring to the history of black slavery		
Repetition of the phrase 'I rise' at the end of the poem		

POETS SPEAKING OUT

The Poem in Context

▌ Working in a small group, discuss where you would put the poem on the continuum lines, below.

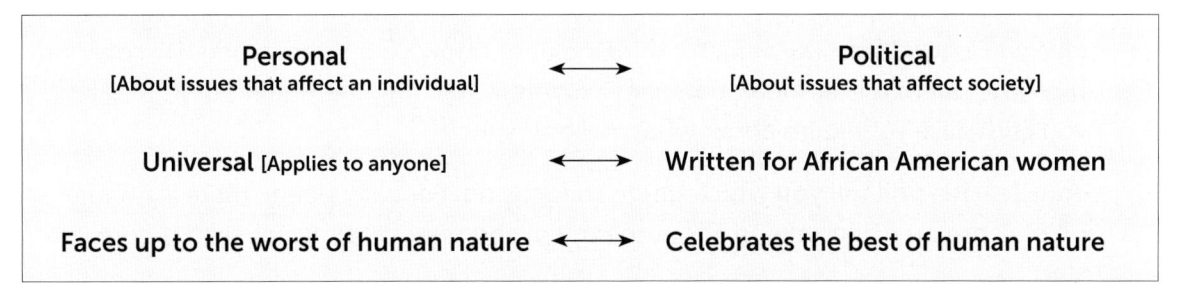

Personal ⟷ **Political**
[About issues that affect an individual]   [About issues that affect society]

Universal [Applies to anyone] ⟷ **Written for African American women**

Faces up to the worst of human nature ⟷ **Celebrates the best of human nature**

▌ In your group, read the two additional pieces of information, below, and discuss whether they change your mind at all about where to place the poem on each continuum.

A. As well as being a writer, Maya Angelou campaigned for equal rights for people of colour and for women. This poem is one of her best known and has often been used to inspire and celebrate the achievements of people of colour, particularly women. For example:
   ▶ An American organization called the UNCF, which helps and encourages African American students to go to college, used the poem in an advertising campaign
   ▶ The BBC used it in their coverage of Wimbledon, with tennis player Serena Williams reading the poem in a montage aired before she won the women's title.

B. Introducing a reading of the poem, Angelou said:
   Everyone in the world has gone to bed one night or another with fear or pain or loss or disappointment and yet each of us has awakened, arisen... seen other human beings and said 'Morning, how are you?', 'I'm fine, thanks, and you?' It's amazing. Wherever that spirit abides in the human being, there is the nobleness of the human spirit.

Pulling It All Together – Maya Angelou Speaks Out

▌ Having worked on the poem and thought about how it is written, try writing two sentences about it, to sum up your thinking about how Angelou uses this poem to 'speak out.' You could all start in the same way and see how differently you express your ideas. For example:

   ▶ Maya Angelou speaks out about…

   ▶ She gets her message across by…

▌ Read out all your summaries as a whole class.

When you read other poems that speak out in this section, remember 'Still I Rise' and use it as a 'foil', thinking about what's special and different about the others by comparison.

KS3 POETRY PLUS
Exploring a Selection of Poems That Speak Out

There are multiple ways to speak out in poetry. You are going to explore a few of these ways by ranging across the selection of poems on pages 119-124. You will investigate what one poem speaks out about and how it is written. Your work on 'Still I Rise' will give you a good starting-point for thinking about how your poem works. Discovering that your poem is like Angelou's poem in some ways, but different in others, will help you crystallise your ideas about what makes it special.

Your teacher will tell you which poem to focus on. For each poem, there is a short bit of contextual information about the poem and poet that you will read before you start.

Working With Your Poem

In pairs, work through the following tasks.

- Read the contextual information about your poem on pages 117 and 118.

- Read the poem itself silently on your own.

- Now read it a second time, out loud, either taking turns to read parts or with one of you reading the whole poem. Decide on what tone you think would be most appropriate before you start.

- Discuss your first thoughts about what the poem is speaking about and how well you think it does this.

- Talk about anything that leaps out at you about the way it is written – one or two things at most that really strike you about how it 'speaks out' about an issue.

POETS SPEAKING OUT

What's Special About Your Poem – Using 'Still I Rise' as a Foil

You've done some initial thinking about your poem and how it works. Now you're going to step back and consider what's special about it, using the Maya Angelou poem as a point of comparison. For instance, if you described Maya Angelou's way of speaking out as being sassy, or celebratory, would you use similar or different adjectives to describe your new poem?

- With your partner, think back to what you decided about 'Still I Rise' and make a list – as long as you can – of everything you notice about your poem in relation to Maya Angelou's poem. (Keep looking back at the two poems, to help you come up with fresh ideas). Don't worry about organising your list at this stage – just come up with as many ideas as you can!

For example, you might find yourself listing these kinds of things:

- Like 'Still I Rise', our poem is about people overcoming difficulties.
- Our poem ends up being uplifting like 'Still I Rise'.
- Unlike 'Still I Rise', the tone of our poem is humorous and light-hearted.
- Our poem has a first person voice, like 'Still I Rise'.

And so on.

- When you've run out of ideas, look at this list to remind yourself of the aspects of poetry that you might have forgotten to think about and add any fresh ideas to your own list:
    - Tone
    - Word choices
    - Figurative language
    - Patterns or broken patterns, for example rhyme, rhythm, repetition
    - The way the poem is structured
    - Voice
    - Layout on the page and line breaks.

- Now join up with another pair who have been looking at the same poem as you. Together, read through your lists and compare what you have said. Add or adapt your lists as you talk and discover new things.

- Using your lists, select the five or six things that you think are the most important and interesting aspects of what your poem has to say and how it says it.

KS3 POETRY PLUS

Writing Critically About a Poem

You should now have some good ideas about what is special about both 'Still I Rise' and the other poem you looked at.

▌ Write a critical piece about either poem, using the title below.

'A Poem that Speaks Out – What it Has to Say and How it Says It'

(For an extra challenge you could write about both 'Still I Rise' and your second poem, comparing the two.)

Writing Your Own Poem

▌ Write your own poem speaking out. You could do it in your own way, choosing a topic that you feel strongly about, or you could use one of these ideas, based on the poems you have been reading:

- ▶ Inspired by 'The Weight' on page 119, write a short poem with one of these titles: 'Don't Throw Your Weight Around' or 'I Feel Weighed Down By…'

- ▶ Use the opening phrases of each line of 'Hijab Scene #7' on page 120 to write your own poem about being stereotyped. It could be stereotypes of gender, or age, or what someone like you is interested in, or anything else you feel strongly about.

No, I'm not	Yes, I
No, I'm not	Yes, I
No, I would not	And if you don't
I'm already	

- ▶ Write a poem of your own, like 'Refugees' on page 124, which can be read from top to bottom or from bottom to top, giving two possible meanings. (If that's too hard, try writing a poem which starts one way but, by the end, reveals something completely different and surprising.)

- ▶ Write a poem like Hollie McNish's poem about politicians on page 122, in which you express your ideas about one of these three groups, by imitating the kind of things they might say or do: school bullies, advertisers of fizzy drinks or chocolate to young children or people who deny that there is global warning.

- ▶ Ask a question that you feel strongly about, like in 'Harlem [2]' on page 121, for instance, 'What's happening to our planet?' or 'What happens when you feel ignored?' Write a poem which, like 'Harlem [2]', carries on asking more questions around that issue, or alternatively, gives five possible responses to the initial question you chose.

POETS SPEAKING OUT

Contextual Information About the Poems

Maryam Hussein: 'The Weight' (on page 119)

Maryam Hussein wrote 'The Weight' when she was a student at Lilian Baylis Technology School. She was one of a group of five or six girls of Somali origin who attended a residential writing course in Devon run by Arvon, as part of a '(M)Other tongue' project. The young people were encouraged to talk and write both in their own home language and in English, and draw on the poetic traditions in their home languages. The poem was written in response to one of the tasks set by the tutors. Maryam talks in the voice of a persona, rather than writing directly about her own personal experience. The poem was published in 2014 in a collection called *Beautiful Like a Traffic Light*.

Mohja Kahf: 'Hijab Scene #7' (on page 120)

Mohja Kahf is a poet who was born in Damascus, Syria and grew up in the Midwest, after her family emigrated to the United States in 1971. She has a PhD in comparative literature and her poems draw on traditions of both Syrian and American poetry. In an interview she talked about the bullying she experienced as an Arabic Muslim girl attending a school in the Midwest. She said:

I remember the actual moment and day when I knew how not to take it anymore… and to whirl around and say something back, and to have that shock of, 'oh, what I say can actually be effective in some way'. That voice is still in me.

Langston Hughes: 'Harlem [2]' (on page 121)

Langston Hughes wrote this poem in 1951. He was a member of the Harlem Renaissance, a group of black writers and artists living in the black ghetto area of New York called Harlem. These writers and artists were part of the Civil Rights Movement that was seeking to end all forms of discrimination against black people in America, including legal segregation (physical separation and separate provision) in schools, hospitals and on buses. Legally enforced public segregation was only finally abolished in the Civil Rights Act of 1964.

Hollie McNish: 'Politicians' (on page 122)

Hollie McNish is one of our most successful and popular contemporary young poets. She has written five books of poetry, all published since 2015 and has released an album of spoken word and music. She won the Ted Hughes Award for Poetry in 2017. Many of her YouTube videos have gone viral. Though known as a performance poet, she said in an interview in the *Guardian* in 2017 that she is 'first and foremost somebody who writes things down', reading her poems from the page at events rather than knowing them off by heart or improvising, like a rap artist. She wrote the poem 'Politicians' when she was 18 years old.

Brian Bilston: 'Refugees' (on page 124)

Brian Bilston is a contemporary poet who tweets his poems regularly.

This poem has been retweeted and 'liked' thousands of times since it first appeared on his Twitterfeed in September 2016. It has been reprinted on *The Huffington Post* and *Independent* websites, read aloud at poetry and charity events and illustrated by artists. Brian Bilston, in one tweet, describes it as a 'forwardy-backwardy' poem, joking that 'forwardy-backwardy' is a technical poetic term! This comment gives you a clue about reading the poem – you really need to get to the end and follow the instructions before you make any judgements about it.

The Weight

I remember the first time I held a gun;
my cousin told me not to touch it.
It was an evil and malicious thing;
dark brown and the sun bounced off it
like oiled skin at the beach,
polished into a blazing sun.
It was heavy.
I dared myself to move. I'd seen its bullets before.

They looked like hand-held coffins;
the gold tips, a silk-lined open casket.

I tried to pick up the Kalashnikov.
It was something new; I was not afraid
but I wasn't strong enough to carry it.
It was heavy,
weighted down by
all those people's lives taken,
all those futures gone for good.
I hear their whispers and cries haunting me,
feel the air thicken,
feel the world evaporating around me.
Silence screams at me.

Maryam Hussein

Hijab Scene #7

No, I'm not bald under the scarf
No, I'm not from that country
where women can't drive cars
No, I would not like to defect
I'm already American
But thank you for offering
What else do you need to know
relevant to my buying insurance,
opening a bank account,
reserving a seat on a flight?
Yes, I speak English
Yes, I carry explosives
They're called words
And if you don't get up
Off your assumptions
They're going to blow you away

Mohja Kahf

Harlem [2]

What happens to a dream deferred?

    Does it dry up
    like a raisin in the sun?
    Or fester like a sore –
    And then run?
    Does it stink like rotten meat?
    Or crust and sugar over –
    like a syrupy sweet?

    Maybe it just sags
    like a heavy load.

Or does it explode?

Langston Hughes

Politicians

Hear hear, ra ra ra
Jolly jolly, fa fa fa
Yes yes, no no,
First speaker – you may go

Bla bla bla, I'm such a toff
Ya ya, cough cough
Fa fa fa, I'm very rich
Jolly jolly, twitch twitch

Bla bla bla 'A better year'
Knock knock 'hear hear'
Fa fa fa 'turn things around'
Clap clap. Sit down

Clap clap. Next one on
Bla bla. He's wrong
Fa fa fa pause pause
'I'm right'. Big applause

Bla bla I've got 6 cars
Jolly jolly fa fa
Pause pause. Wait wait
Cough cough. Kids are great

Bla bla big applause
Fa fa 'better laws'
'Hear hear' bench taps
Sit down. Clap clap

POETS SPEAKING OUT

Next one up 'I don't agree'
Ra ra 'Vote for me'
Bla bla 'cos I can'
bang my fists down like a man

Ya ya well I can lean
Ra ra to make it seem
like what I say is really good
Clap clap. Tap the wood

I wave my hand up in the air
to make it look like you should care
or point my finger round instead
to give some worth to what I've said

Bla bla 'I see I see'
Good Lord! In fact you're just like me
You're dull, you're grey, you're almost dead
You never did those things you said

You 'want us equal, want fair rules'
and send your kids to public schools
you moan about 'the country's state'
books for schools, the time you wait

in hospitals, the lack of care
although *you* don't get treated there
you promise them you have a plan
but you've stretched the budget all you can

'There's no more money left' you say
'Except all that, but that's my pay'
'Jolly show, I'm just like you
– are you a politician too?'

Hollie McNish (written aged 18)

KS3 POETRY PLUS

(WARNING: Don't judge this poem until you have read the whole thing.)

Refugees

They have no need of our help
So do not tell me
These haggard faces could belong to you or me
Should life have dealt a different hand
We need to see them for who they really are
Chancers and scroungers
Layabouts and loungers
With bombs up their sleeves
Cut-throats and thieves
They are not
Welcome here
We should make them
Go back to where they came from
They cannot
Share our food
Share our homes
Share our countries
Instead let us
Build a wall to keep them out
It is not okay to say
These are people just like us
A place should only belong to those who are born there
Do not be so stupid to think that
The world can be looked at another way

(now read from bottom to top)

Brian Bilston

POEMS ON THE THEME OF LOVE

KS3 POETRY PLUS
POEMS ON THE THEME OF LOVE

In this unit, you will:

▶ Read a selection of poems about love

▶ Explore the different ways in which poets write about love

▶ Compare poems which make us look afresh at love and love poetry.

Starting to Think About Love Poems – Thinking Broadly

The first three lines from each of the poems in this unit are included on page 127.

■ Working in small groups, begin by reading them all out loud and sharing your first thoughts on the similarities and differences between them.

■ To help you think further about the similarities and differences between the poems, sort the extracts in as many different ways as you can. You could begin by trying some of the groupings suggested here, then come up with your own. (Don't get stuck on one way of connecting the extracts – keep creating new groupings.)

▶ **The subject and the angle taken**, for example poems about love generally and poems describing a loved one

▶ **Tone**, for example poems which are serious and those which are light-hearted or those which seem happy and those which seem sad

▶ **Type of language**, for example poems that sound conversational and those which sound poetic or those which use language in conventional ways and those which do something unusual

▶ **Use of imagery**, for example those which use poetic techniques such as similes and metaphors and those that don't

▶ **Voice**, for example poems written in the first person ('I'), or those which address a listener ('you') or even simply poems where there is something unusual or striking about the voice versus those that are about third-person voices.

■ Take it in turns to share your findings in class feedback. You might choose to report on a particular way of grouping the extracts or on an extract you have discovered something interesting about. For example, an extract which fitted into different groupings or one which didn't have many connections with the other extracts.

POEMS ON THE THEME OF LOVE

| 1 | My mistress' eyes are nothing like the sun;
Coral is far more red than her lips' red;
If snow be white, why then her breasts are dun; |

| 2 | How do I love thee? Let me count the ways.
I love thee to the depth and breadth and height
My soul can reach, when feeling out of sight |

| 3 | Had I the heavens' embroidered cloths,
Enwrought with golden and silver light,
The blue and the dim and the dark cloths |

| 4 | Have you forgotten what we were like then
when we were still first rate
and the day came fat with an apple in its mouth |

| 5 | without any assistance or guidance from you
i have loved you assiduously for 8 months 2 wks & a day
i have been stood up four times |

| 6 | Come when the nights are bright with stars
Or come when the moon is mellow;
Come when the sun his golden bars |

| 7 | Please marrow me, my beloved sweetpea,
so that we may beetroot to our hearts.
Lettuce have the courgette of our convictions |

| 8 | that on the last day of july
my father would tell the story
of how they had met |

| 9 | O my Luve is like a red, red rose
  That's newly sprung in June;
O my Luve is like the melody |

KS3 POETRY PLUS

A Recipe For Love?

- As a class, talk about what you expect from a love poem. Together see if you can come up with a recipe for the 'Classic Poem about Love'. Think about your ingredients and your method for putting them together. Use the ideas below to get you started:

RECIPE

FOR: A CLASSIC POEM ABOUT LOVE
FROM THE KITCHEN OF:
PREP TIME: _____ COOK TIME: _____ SERVES: _____

Ingredients
1. 1 x beloved, more perfect than anyone else

Method
1. Place loved one on pedestal

Included on pages 129-131 are three love poems.

- Listen to the three poems being read out loud.

- As soon as you have heard all three poems and without saying anything to anyone, write for 10 minutes about the poems. Don't worry about what to say – just explore your personal response. For example, you could write about which you liked best, thinking about why this was (the sounds, the pictures it conjures up, the feelings it expresses).

- In groups, share your response, then talk about the different ways in which the poems meet your expectations of a love poem. In what ways do they match your recipe? Are they all good matches, in their own way, or is one more of a 'classic love poem' than the others?

POEMS ON THE THEME OF LOVE

Sonnets from the Portuguese 43: How Do I Love Thee?

How do I love thee? Let me count the ways.
I love thee to the depth and breadth and height
My soul can reach, when feeling out of sight
For the ends of being and ideal grace.
I love thee to the level of every day's
Most quiet need, by sun and candle-light.
I love thee freely, as men strive for right;
I love thee purely, as they turn from praise.
I love thee with the passion put to use
In my old griefs, and with my childhood's faith.
I love thee with a love I seemed to lose
With my lost saints. I love thee with the breath,
Smiles, tears, of all my life; and, if God choose,
I shall but love thee better after death.

Elizabeth Barrett Browning

Invitation to Love

Come when the nights are bright with stars
Or come when the moon is mellow;
Come when the sun his golden bars
Drops on the hay-field yellow.
Come in the twilight soft and gray,
Come in the night or come in the day,
Come, O love, whene'er you may,
And you are welcome, welcome.

You are sweet, O Love, dear Love,
You are soft as the nesting dove.
Come to my heart and bring it to rest
As the bird flies home to its welcome nest.

Come when my heart is full of grief
Or when my heart is merry;
Come with the falling of the leaf
Or with the redd'ning cherry.
Come when the year's first blossom blows,
Come when the summer gleams and glows,
Come with the winter's drifting snows,
And you are welcome, welcome.

Paul Lawrence Dunbar

A Red, Red Rose

O my Luve is like a red, red rose
   That's newly sprung in June;
O my Luve is like the melody
   That's sweetly played in tune.

So fair art thou, my bonnie lass,
   So deep in luve am I;
And I will luve thee still, my dear,
   Till a' the seas gang dry.

Till a' the seas gang dry, my dear,
   And the rocks melt wi' the sun;
I will love thee still, my dear,
   While the sands o' life shall run.

And fare thee weel, my only luve!
   And fare thee weel awhile!
And I will come again, my luve,
   Though it were ten thousand mile.

Robert Burns

KS3 POETRY PLUS

Fresh Angles on Love

As long as poets have been writing love poems, they have also been playing with their readers' and listeners' expectations of what love poetry is. You are going to explore five love poems from across time, all which do something rather unexpected. They might:

- Take aspects of the classic love poem and give them an unusual twist
- Ignore the ingredients of classic love poetry (its conventions) and do something entirely different
- Use the conventions of an entirely different kind of writing and pour in ideas about love.

Exploring a Poem and Presenting It to the Class

You are going to work in groups on just one of the poems (pages 134-137). Your teacher will tell you which one to work on. You will be reading your poem and introducing it to the whole class. Later, the class will choose two of the poems to focus on in more detail.

- Read the poem to yourself, then read it out loud. Share your first responses then work together to help each other understand the poem and what it seems to be saying about love.

- Now read the poem again, this time focusing on what is unusual or surprising about it. Does your poem:
  - Make us look at love in a new way
  - Challenge our expectations of love poetry
  - Both?

- How does it do this? Some of the ways in which poets surprise the reader or make them think freshly about a familiar subject are listed here.

- Unusual spellings and capitalisation
- Unconventional sentence punctuation (or no punctuation at all)
- Strange word order
- New words or words used playfully
- New combinations of well-known phrases
- Unexpected images or new ways of looking at familiar things
- Unexpected angles on the subject or surprising twists.

POEMS ON THE THEME OF LOVE

- As a group, prepare a reading of your poem and a short presentation on what is unusual and special about your love poem.

- Take it in turns to read your poems to the whole class and introduce your ideas about how and why they give a fresh slant to love poetry.

- Working as a class, pull together
    - Anything the five poems have in common
    - Any connections the five poems have with the love poems you explored at the beginning of this unit
    - What makes each of these poems special and distinctive.

Voting on Two Poems to Investigate Further

You have now listened to five poems and heard a bit about each of them.

- As a class, take a vote to agree on two of these poems that you want to investigate in more detail. (Don't be put off from choosing the more surprising, odd or difficult poems. This is a chance for the class to think together, get more familiar with the poems and come up with good ideas.)

On page 138 you will find activities to help you investigate the two poems you have chosen in more detail.

KS3 POETRY PLUS

Fresh Angles on Love – The Poems

He Wishes For the Cloths of Heaven

Had I the heavens' embroidered cloths,
Enwrought with golden and silver light,
The blue and the dim and the dark cloths
Of night and light and the half-light,
I would spread the cloths under your feet:
But I, being poor, have only my dreams;
I have spread my dreams under your feet;
Tread softly because you tread on my dreams.

W.B. Yeats

Love in the Time of Cauliflower

Please marrow me, my beloved sweetpea,
so that we may beetroot to our hearts.
Lettuce have the courgette of our convictions
and our love elevated to Great Artichoke.

Don't leek me feeling this way, my dear,
such lofty asparagus can't be ignored.
I am a prisoner, trapped in your celery;
Don't make me go back to the drawing broad beans.

We all carry emotional cabbage:
love is chard and not inconsequential,
but may our passion be uncucumbered
so that we reach our true potato.

Oh, how your onions make my head spinach,
reduce me to mushrooms, broccoli, defenceless.
Only you can salsify my desire,
and I, in turnip, will radish you senseless.

love poem, inadvertently written with auto-carrot switched on

Brain Bilston

No Assistance

without any assistance or guidance from you
i have loved you assiduously for 8 months 2 wks & a day
i have been stood up four times
i've left 7 packages on yr doorstep
forty poems 2 plants & 3 handmade notecards i left
town so i cd send to you have been no help to me
on my job
you call at 3:00 in the mornin on weekdays
so i cd drive 27½ miles cross the bay before i go to work
charmin charmin
but you are of no assistance
i want you to know
this waz an experiment
to see how selfish i cd be
if i wd really carry on to snare a possible lover
if i waz capable of debasin my self for the love of another
if i cd stand not being wanted
when i wanted to be wanted
& i cannot
so
with no further assistance & no guidance from you
i am endin this affair

this note is attached to a plant
i've been waterin since the day i met you
you may water it
yr damn self

Ntozake Shange

Animals

Have you forgotten what we were like then
when we were still first rate
and the day came fat with an apple in its mouth

it's no use worrying about Time
but we did have a few tricks up our sleeves
and turned some sharp corners

the whole pasture looked like our meal
we didn't need speedometers
we could manage cocktails out of ice and water

I wouldn't want to be faster
or greener than now if you were with me O you
were the best of all my days

Frank O'Hara

the parents anniversary

    that on the last day of july
    my father would tell the story
    of how they had met
    so young in photos i once saw
    of an eighties blurred with rain
    and home haircuts
    how easily she had made
    her impression and left it there
        that years later he would
    follow her to pulsing cities
    and countries now closed
    to the rest of the world
        that they would marry
    dress each other in light
    a day so hot that sand
    could boil to glass
    she, a striped cat who purrs
    he, a tamed bear.
        that they could repeat these words
    a little different year by year
    but by the same stellate night
    that he could sleep in
    the fourth chamber of her heart
    and stay there and stay there

Lucy Thynne

KS3 POETRY PLUS
Investigating the Two Poems You Voted On

- First, you are going to explore each poem in more detail, as a whole class.
- Then, you are going to pool ideas about what makes each one special in relation to each other.
- Finally, you are going to draw on everything you've discussed to write a comparison between the two poems.

The First Poem

- In pairs or threes, read the poem. Think about it in terms of:
  - **The subject and the angle taken**, for example poems about love and poems describing a loved one
  - **Tone**, for example poems which are serious and those which are light-hearted or those which seem happy and those which seem sad
  - **Type of language**, for example poems that sound conversational and those which sound poetic or those which use language in conventional ways and those which do something unusual
  - **Use of imagery**, for example those which use poetic techniques such as similes and those that don't
  - **Voice**, for example poems written in the first person ('I'), or those which address a listener ('you') or even simply poems where there is something unusual or striking about the voice.

- Now choose three ideas to bring to a whole class discussion:
  - The one thing that you think is most special and interesting about this poem and how it deals with the theme of love (for example, something to do with the tone, use of imagery, voice or something else)
  - One thing that you really like about the poem
  - One thing that you'd like to ask your teacher and/or classmates about the poem. It should be something that you wish you could make more sense of, or think might raise interesting ideas in discussion.

- Talk about the poem as a whole class, by getting different groups to raise their ideas and questions for discussion.

POEMS ON THE THEME OF LOVE

The Second Poem

▌ Your teacher will talk to you about this poem. This time, they will explain their thoughts about what makes it especially interesting and will raise with you any questions or aspects that they're not sure about, or where they have alternative ideas about how it might be read.

While your teacher is talking, jot down any ideas you have, either in response to what they say, or where you have a different idea. Jot down thoughts in answer to any questions they have.

▌ As a whole class, respond to your teacher's ideas and questions, asking questions of your own if you want to.

Comparing the Poems – What Makes Them Interesting and Unusual

Now you have a good sense of the two poems, it's time to compare them. This will help you think about what connects the two poems and will give you an even better understanding of what makes each poem special and distinctive.

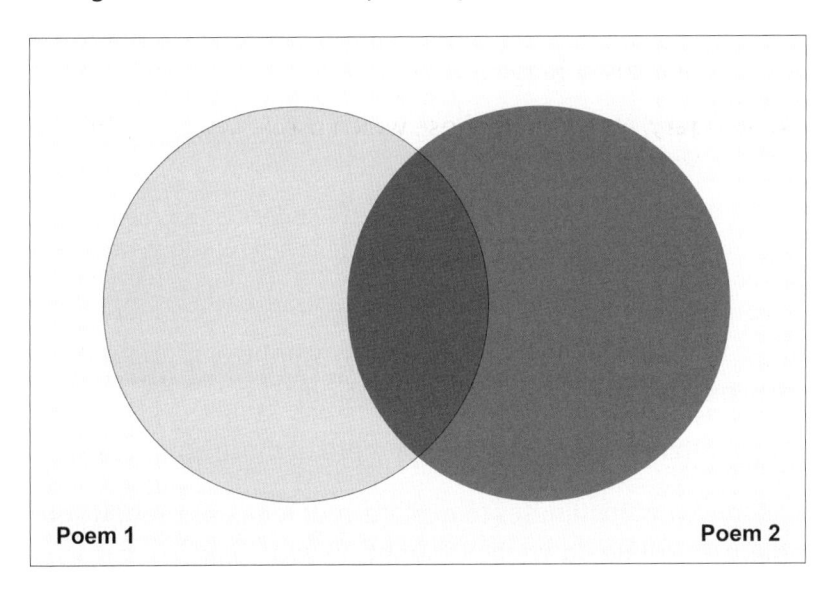

[Venn diagram with two overlapping circles labelled "Poem 1" and "Poem 2"]

▌ On a large sheet of paper, draw a Venn diagram with overlapping circles, like the one above. Write the name of your poems underneath each circle.

The question you are going to explore is:

| How do poem 1 and poem 2 give a fresh angle on love and love poetry? |

KS3 POETRY PLUS

- In pairs, begin by considering the statements below. Do they apply to one or both of the poems? If just to one, write it in the circle for that poem. If it seems relevant to both, write it in the overlapping section.

- Pause and think about the two poems again. Is there anything else you want to say about either or both of them? If so, write your own statements and place them on the Venn diagram.

1. Uses imagery that is unconventional for love poetry.
2. Uses humour to be playful and entertaining rather than serious about love.
3. Expresses conventional ideas about love but in an unusual style.
4. Makes a serious point about love.
5. Uses unusual punctuation to express something important about the love described.
6. Uses familiar words and phrases but in new and unusual ways.
7. Plays with our expectations of what love poetry is.
8. Uses layout to surprise the reader and challenge their expectations.
9. Introduces surreal or fantastical images or goes into flights of fancy.
10. Expects the reader to work hard to know what is going on.

You now need to think about what you actually want to say about the poems in answer to the question you've been investigating!

- Work out your thinking by trying one or more of these approaches:

  ▶ Write for five or ten minutes to explore your ideas, as though you were writing in a diary or writing down the thoughts in your head. Then read over what you have written – or read it to someone else – to see if you have worked out your angle on the question.

  ▶ In pairs, take it in turns to explore your thinking, using the phrase 'What I want to say is this…' to get you started.

  ▶ Review the statements on your Venn diagram and try out different ways of arranging them.

- Do your piece of writing. (You could give it to someone else to look at to suggest any changes or improvements before writing a final version.)

POEMS ON THE THEME OF LOVE

Reflecting on a Piece of Comparative Writing

Having written your own comparison, you are now going to read and discuss an essay written by a teacher comparing 'Animals,' with a sonnet called 'Time Does Not Bring Relief'. The two poems are included on page 142.

- Read both poems and with a partner share your ideas about them in relation to each other.

- Now talk about how you might go about comparing them, if you were writing about them. For instance:
    - What kinds of things would be most interesting to compare
    - How might you structure your comparison
    - Which poem would you start with?

- Now read the comparison.

- Make a list of bullet points about anything you find interesting in what this writer says about the two poems and what you think she does well (or less well) in the way she goes about the comparison.

- Share your ideas as a class.

- Look back at your own comparison of the two poems you studied as a class and reflect on anything you might do differently next time you write a comparative essay.

Time Does Not Bring Relief

Time does not bring relief; you all have lied
Who told me time would ease me of my pain!
I miss him in the weeping of the rain;
I want him at the shrinking of the tide;
The old snows melt from every mountain-side,
And last year's leaves are smoke in every lane;
But last year's bitter loving must remain
Heaped on my heart, and my old thoughts abide.
There are a hundred places where I fear
To go,—so with his memory they brim.
And entering with relief some quiet place
Where never fell his foot or shone his face
I say, 'There is no memory of him here!'
And so stand stricken, so remembering him.

Edna St Vincent Millay

Animals

Have you forgotten what we were like then
when we were still first rate
and the day came fat with an apple in its mouth

it's no use worrying about Time
but we did have a few tricks up our sleeves
and turned some sharp corners

the whole pasture looked like our meal
we didn't need speedometers
we could manage cocktails out of ice and water

I wouldn't want to be faster
or greener than now if you were with me O you
were the best of all my days

Frank O'Hara

POEMS ON THE THEME OF LOVE

An Example: Comparing 'Animals' and 'Time Does Not Bring Relief'

Both poems are reflecting back on a past love, with some sense of regret. The focus of 'Animals' is the simplicity of this lost love and it is addressed directly to the former partner. Some of the shared memories in the poem seem very personal and hard to pin down, but the speaker definitely seems to look back longingly. The focus of the second poem is different, as it's about the speaker's total devastation following the loss of a loved one (either death or separation, we're not sure). It is written in present tense, which seems to add to the totality of the pain the speaker is feeling and helps us to feel it with them.

The poems are similar in the way that memories play a big part in creating emotion. The speaker in 'Animals' portrays an idyllic past life where nothing was complicated: 'the whole pasture was our meal' and 'we could manage cocktails out of ice and water', which suggests their youthfulness. The speaker in 'Time Does Not Bring Relief' also focuses on memories. The speaker says 'There are a hundred places where I fear/To go' as the memories are too raw and painful and it seems like everything makes her think of her lover: 'the weeping of the rain', 'the shrinking of the tide', which almost suggests that the speaker is afraid to go outside for fear of being reminded of her memories with him.

In both poems the speakers seem to wish for their love back, although in 'Animals' it is less obviously stated. In 'Time Does Not Bring Relief', the speaker actually tells us she is 'stricken' every time she remembers her loved one and doesn't like going to places where there are memories or where there are no memories, which covers all the places she could go. She says 'last year's bitter loving must remain/Heaped on my heart, and my old thoughts abide.'

Though both poems are similar in these ways, they also have many important differences. The speaker in 'Animals' does not seem to be very bitter about the loss of the loved one and seems to accept it as a time gone by whereas the speaker in 'Time' is incredibly bitter and even accuses the people who try to console her of being liars when they tell her she will get better.

Of the two poems, the one I found most interesting was 'Animals'. I liked the way the poet really captured a sense of young, innocent love where complicated aspects of adult relationships didn't matter. It is sad, because the speaker still feels like these were the best days, but unlike 'Time Does Not Bring Relief' he is not angry about this. I liked the interesting use of imagery with phrases like 'turned some sharp corners' and 'cocktails' which made me think of bright scenes from a film.

Lucy Hinchliffe

KS3 POETRY PLUS
Your Own Fresh Angle on a Love Poem

- Use what you have learned about the way poets make familiar topics fresh again and give a new spin to traditional ideas to write your own quirky love poem. Your aim is to take your reader by surprise or make them think differently about love, love poetry or both.

You could:

- Follow Brian Bilston's lead and play with the language of love – why not use fruit instead of vegetables? For example:

    If only we could spend the rest of our limes in lemon!

    Limes = lives
    Lemon = heaven

- Mix together standard English and the language you use with friends or at home

- Use capitalisation, bold lettering, italics, underlinings or other design features to emphasise your meaning

- Invent new metaphors and similes or combine familiar phrases in new and strange ways

- Invent new words

- Play with the way you use punctuation – or don't use any at all

- Use line breaks or spacing inventively to help convey the meaning you want to get across.

- Write a short reflection on your poem and the way you have played with language to create particular effects or get your meaning across.

- Share your new angles on love as:

    - An 'open mic' performance session

    - A gallery of poems and reflections

    - An anthology of poems and reflections.

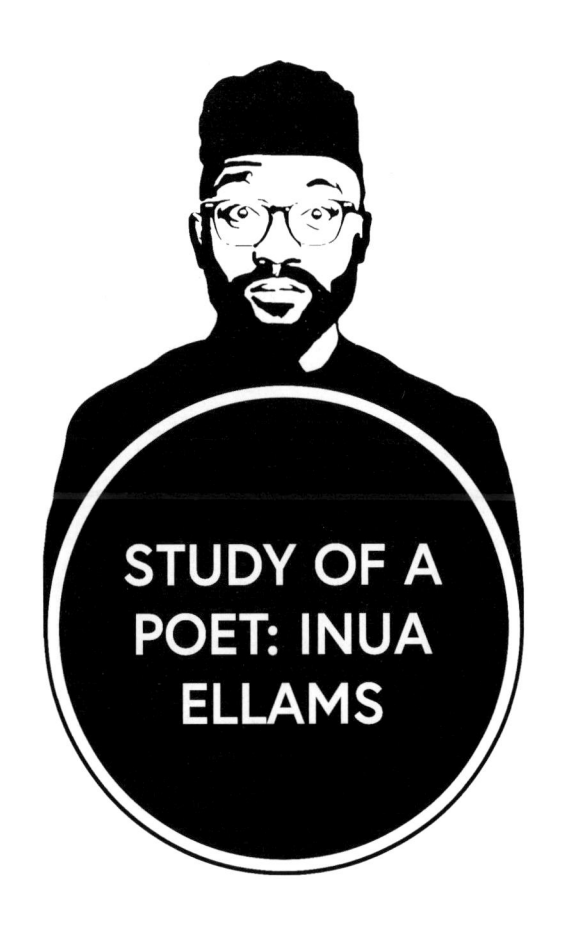

STUDY OF A POET: INUA ELLAMS

KS3 POETRY PLUS
STUDY OF A POET – INUA ELLAMS

In this section you will study several poems by the same poet and have the opportunity to explore what's special about his approach to poetry. Inua Ellams writes poems and plays and is also a performer, graphic artist and designer. He was born in Nigeria in 1984 and sees himself as a poet of the hip hop generation. You will have a chance to think about how these things have influenced his poetry.

You can watch Inua Ellams reading his poetry on the EMC website.

'Dear Tina'

Making Predictions

All the words and phrases on page 147 come from the same poem.

- Share out the word collections in groups of three or four around the class.

- In your group, read the words you have been allocated and share your first impressions and ideas. For example, why might these words have been grouped together? What do the words make you think or feel? What do you notice or find interesting?

- In your group, make some predictions about the poem these words came from. For example, where and when it might take place? Who and what it is about? (Bear in mind that your ideas might change a lot when you hear more words from the poem, and then see the poem itself.)

- Share ideas across the class about your different word collections.

- As a class, make some new predictions now that you have heard about a wider range of words and phrases from the poem.

STUDY OF A POET: INUA ELLAMS

Word collections

Group A	Group B
crying	embrace
dodging	kiss
found	he followed
hiding	never let go
lost	peacefully
screaming	promising
wailing	romances
	sailed her away
	welcoming

Group C	Group D
hurricane lamp	90 years
into rain	all these years
jungle	an hour after
Paris	pass like minutes
Rome	the day
sailed her away	the past
through rain	too fast
urban jungle	

Group E	Group F
anti-hero	digital codes
bullets	ones and zeros
civil war	text message
died	too fast
drop zones	urban jungle
hero	wifi zones
Morse code	X Factor
peacefully	
survived	

KS3 POETRY PLUS

Words and Phrases in Context (1)

In the previous activity, you were looking at words and phrases out of context. You are now going to look at how these words and phrases are used in the poem, so be alert to surprises and the unexpected.

- Either listen to Inua Ellams introduce and read 'Dear Tina' or listen as your teacher reads it. You can follow along on page 149.

- Discuss how the poem compares to the predictions you made before reading. If there were surprises, or ways in which your predictions went in a completely different direction from the poem, look particularly closely at how these words and phrases appear in the context of the poem and discuss what you notice.

- Working in the group you were in for the 'Making Predictions' activity, above, discuss your first impressions of the poem.

- Working in your group, read the poem again, looking out for the words and phrases you looked at earlier in the context of the whole poem.

- Discuss what you notice now about how Ellams has used these words and phrases in the poem.

- As a class, share your ideas about your word collections.

- As a class, look again at all the word collections and see what you notice, for example contrasts or words that appear in different groupings.

STUDY OF A POET: INUA ELLAMS

Dear Tina

The day I discovered how she survived the civil war,
how she saw her friends pass like minutes into oblivion,
how she screamed through drop zones and Morse codes
into jungle, dodging bullets, hiding and crying into rain,

the day I discovered my grandfather heard her wailing,
felt something enough to move him after her, in darkness,
through rain, how her eyes, found in the flickering bounce
of hurricane lamps, showed a place so pure, he sailed her

away to the embrace of Paris, the kiss of Rome, the world
with its wide welcoming dome. The day I discovered this,
why she called him hero, she died. Peacefully, 90 years old.
He followed an hour after, again into darkness.

All those years, he never let go. That day, I realised we live
in different worlds; friends pass too fast for minutes, wars
come after X Factor, turtle dove romances exist in the past.

But I will send one sentence to you. One text message
screaming through wifi zones, digital codes, dodging
ones and zeros, like bullets and anti-heroes, promising

if evr ur lst n ths urbn jngle,
i'll fnd n brng u in frm rain.

KS3 POETRY PLUS

Words and Phrases in Context (2)

- Working individually, you are going to create a concept map for 'Dear Tina'. To do this:

    - Choose one of the words or phrases in the collection you have been investigating and write it in the middle of the page.

    - Now draw a line to connect it to another word or phrase from the poem. You can make connections between the words in the group you have been investigating, but go further than that as well, to make connections across the whole poem.

    - Along the line, write an explanation of the link you have made. An example has been done for you, below.

    - Keep going, connecting your word to as many others as you can.

- Share your concept map with others in your predictions group. Discuss some of the similarities and differences in the ways you have made connections across the poem.

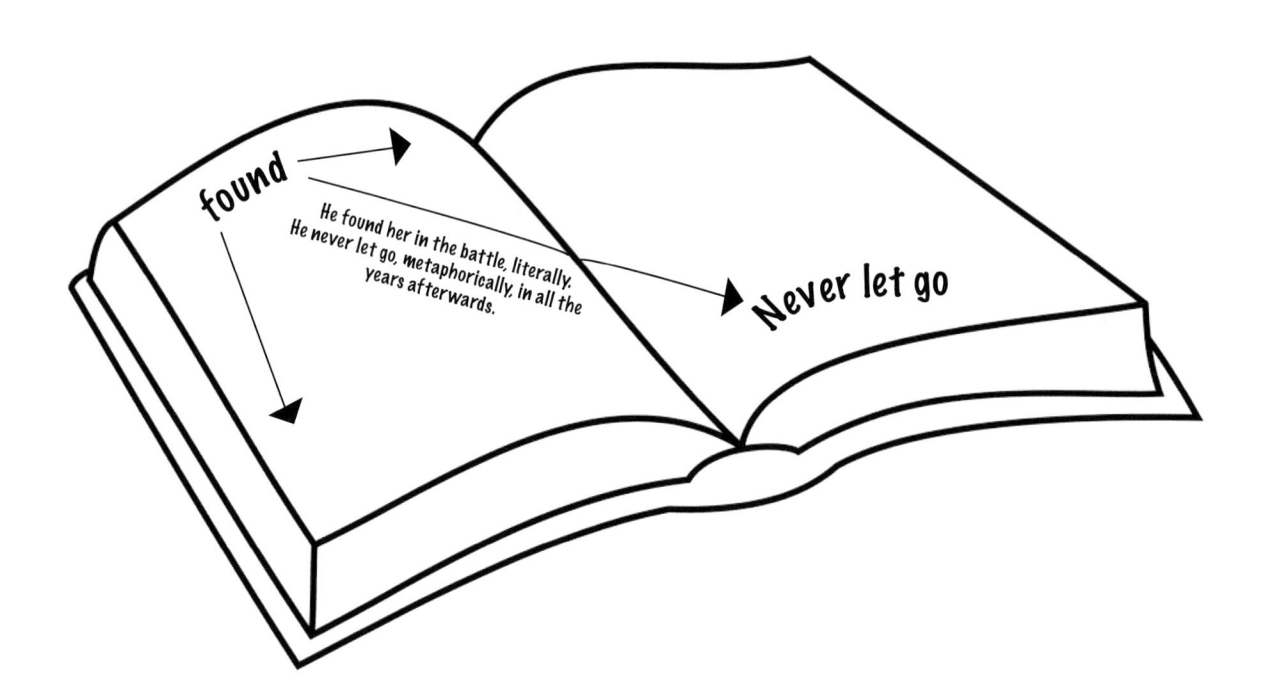

found →

He found her in the battle, literally.
He never let go, metaphorically, in all the years afterwards.

→ *Never let go*

STUDY OF A POET: INUA ELLAMS

Over to You – The Remix

Inua Ellams says in his introduction to 'Dear Tina':

> 'Dear Tina' is sort of half stolen, half my story. One of the most interesting things about being a child of the hip hop generation is figuring out how it has influenced me, in subtle and unsubtle ways. And one of the strongest elements of hip hop culture and music is re-mixing. One of the things I do as a poet is to remix my life with the lives of others. So the first half of the poem is a story someone gave to me, who I met late one night at a poetry reading in Brixton, and it fitted perfectly with stories of my own grandparents. This poem is an amalgamation of those two things. But it's also very personal. It's a love poem which I sent to someone I was dating, long distance, called Tina.

▌ You are going to write a poem of your own, using the idea of 'remixing'. You could:

- Borrow elements of the poem 'Dear Tina' to write Tina's reply, titled 'Dear Inua'
- Create a poem by mixing the story in 'Dear Tina' with a story from your own life
- Choose two or more of the poems from the Anthology (pages 169-220) and remix them into a new poem
- Create a poem by mixing a story from your own life with a story you have heard from someone else's life.

KS3 POETRY PLUS

'Ghetto van Gogh'

Before reading the next poem, it is useful to know that it references a painter, Vincent van Gogh, whose self-portrait is pictured here. He is famous for his paintings, but also for an episode of madness in which he cut off part of his own ear during an argument with a close friend.

Poetry or Prose?

You are now going to explore a prose poem called 'Ghetto van Gogh'. A prose poem is a piece of imaginative, poetic writing in prose.

- Read Ghetto van Gogh on page 153.

- Discuss the poem as a whole class, focusing on the following questions:
    - ▶ What is the poem about?
    - ▶ What message does the poem contain?
    - ▶ Why does the poem mention mouths and ears so much? What might Ellams want his readers to think?
    - ▶ What do you think about the ending of the poem?
    - ▶ Where would you place it on the continuum line, below, to show whether you think it is poetry, prose or a mixture of the two? Why?

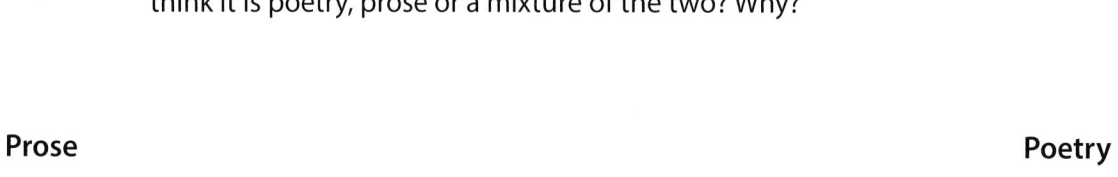

Vincent Van Gogh

Prose   Poetry

STUDY OF A POET: INUA ELLAMS

Ghetto van Gogh

The night my mother tells the story of the thief I am cross-legged on her lap. Her mouth is inches from my ear. She lets the dusk slip into her voice and whispers about the boy who snatched a mango at the market and ran, becoming the teenager who robbed a shop at gun point, shot the blind cashier, shot him as he fell, shot him once more dead; became the man who stole 36 cars and when apprehended, to be publicly hanged, asked for one wish, his whole lip quivering.

My mother who is inches from my ear, explains his dying wish to speak to his mother. The crowd parted silently, she gathered his bound wrists, kissed his rough skin, her cheeks shimmering in the killing heat. He bent forward, says mother, her mouth even closer, dusky voice hushed, bent towards her cheek as if to kiss goodbye and switched sharply, bit into her ear, strained against the flesh, ripped the thing off and spat / you should have told me mother, what I did was wrong /.

Arguing the Case

- Write a print or online magazine review of 'Ghetto van Gogh' in which you argue strongly that it is or is not a poem. You should consider some of the elements of poetry summarised below, when planning your response:

What makes a poem a poem?

A. Published in a poetry book

B. Strong emotional impact

C. Memorable vocabulary

D. Figurative language – metaphor, simile, personification, hyperbole, and so on

E. Patterned language – patterns made and patterns broken

F. Condensed language

G. Focus on lay out – line breaks, lay-out, verses, and so on

H. Shows the possibilities of language

I. Makes readers look at the world in unusual ways

KS3 POETRY PLUS

'Summit of Flight'

Mother Means Well

'Mother means well' is a phrase that is repeated three times in the next poem you are going to read, 'Summit of Flight'.

- As a class, tell any stories you have about a parent or other adult who gave you well-meaning advice but who just doesn't understand what it's like to be a child or teenager today.

- Next listen to Inua Ellams introduce and read the 'Summit of Flight', or listen as your teacher reads it. You can follow along on pages 156-157. Listen out in particular for the phrase 'Mother means well'.

- You probably won't have a clear sense of what the poem is about from a single reading of it. Based on your first impressions, discuss why you think Ellams repeats the phrase 'Mother means well' three times. Why do you think the final response of the narrator is 'You just won't understand' and why is it made 'softly'?

A Poem About…

- You are now going to read the poem closely on your own, trying to work out what you think it is about. Spend 10 minutes thinking and jotting down ideas on your own.

- When you have done this, write about the poem, following the structure below. After each stage, share some of your sentences as a class and discuss any similarities and differences in your ideas about the poem and what you have chosen to write.

- After writing and sharing your sentences about the poem, discuss how your thoughts were influenced by hearing what other people said.

> **Stage 1: This poem is about…**
> ▶ Write a single sentence summary of the poem, beginning 'This poem is about…'
>
> **Stage 2: Adding to your sentence**
> ▶ On your own, add to your sentence so that it reads 'This poem is about… and…'
>
> **Stage 3: A further comment**
> ▶ Add a final comment to your sentence about the poem.

STUDY OF A POET: INUA ELLAMS

Poem to Film

▌ Imagine you have been asked to turn this poem into a short film. Working with a partner, you are going to use a storyboard template like this one to plan your film.

A picture of what you see on screen		
Sound		

Each box shows a shot from your film (what will be seen on screen) and underneath you will write any sound, including dialogue, sound effects and music. You will need to discuss the points, below.

- Will you have a narrator?
- Will you have any dialogue?
- What sound effects will you use?
- Will you have any background music?
- Will the mother appear on screen?
- What lines will you use from the poem?
- What do you think Ellams is trying to show about the speaker's feelings as he packs up his basket ball kit? How will you put this across in your film?
- Ellams uses some interesting images in his poem. For example: the 'throat of my sneakers'; the 'towel like a dead body'; the 'large onion'; the 'lines and circles' of the basket ball court in his mind's eye as he leaves; the ball spinning like a world. Will you actually show any of these images on film, or just the people and what they are doing? If so, which ones and why? If not, why not?
- How will you use the camera to bring out important aspects of the poem. For example, when will you use a close up to focus on a specific image? When will you use a long shot to show the bigger picture?

▌ When you've finished your storyboard, talk about what you've learned about the poem by doing this kind of work on it. For instance:

- Do you now remember some lines better than others?
- Has it made you notice anything new about the poem? For example, how much or how little is about setting a scene in his home? How much speech there is?

Summit of Flight

Mother means well. She is in the next room
but knows I'm crushing socks into balls
of white cotton and shoving them down
the throat of my sneakers as she shouts
/ Are you off to play that game again? /

When I don't answer but squeeze and roll
my old towel till it's silent and forlorn
like a dead body I lift into the black bag,
she wants to know / Why not football
like everybody else. /

Mother means well but I wring the neck
of my water bottle when she yells
/ Even rugby is better than throwing
a large onion into a basket like a girl
in a market, it's a game for girls /

STUDY OF A POET: INUA ELLAMS

she says as I twist two sweat bands
like wrists into my back pocket
/ Sailing, cycling, anything else, but
you had to pick what no one cares
about, what kind of kid does that? /

Mother means well, as I shoulder the bag
and stare down the summit of flight
of stairs imagining the many routes out
of the house, each one a multitude
of lines and circles – perfect geometry

on which to forge my path. I stay low,
five strides and I've passed each creak
and crevice, pivoted on the last step,
edged the sharp desk onto the carpet,
nimbling towards the door

without a sound or uttered word,
only the human breath pushed down
the tangled line of tendon, muscle, bone
and the human spirit's strive to lift it all,
all the while spinning the ball like a world,

a lone star on a fingertip, out on a limb,
brighter for all the empty darkness around it,
floating through the door. Before it slams
Mother asks why I play the game. I respond
softly / You just won't understand /

KS3 POETRY PLUS

'Directions'

Copying, Borrowing or Stealing?

Plagiarism is very much frowned upon in the literary world and defined in the *Oxford Dictionary* as:

> The practice of taking someone else's work or ideas and passing them off as one's own.

However, there is also a long tradition of poets borrowing ideas and even whole lines from each other, writing in response to another poet's work and so on.

▪ Working with a partner, re-read what Inua Ellams says about 'remixing' on page 151 and then read what American poet Billy Collins writes in his poem 'The Trouble with Poetry', below.

> … the longing to steal,
> to break into the poems of others
> with a flashlight and a ski mask.
> And what an unmerry band of thieves we are,
> cut-purses, common shoplifters

▪ As a class, discuss what you think Collins and Ellams are saying about the process of writing a poem.

▪ With your partner, discuss the questions, below, to help you to decide what is acceptable and when it is not – when the 'stealing' becomes 'plagiarism'.

- ▶ What (rough) percentage of a poem do you think could be borrowed from another, as long as it was used in a different way and mixed with the poet's own language and ideas? 0%? 10%? 30%? What about 50%? Or 70%? Or even 90%?

- ▶ Would it be acceptable to:
    - Take an idea or a theme, but give it a new slant?
    - Write on exactly the same idea or theme, using a lot of the same words and phrases?
    - Use another poet's phrases, but give them your own twist?
    - Use whole lines?
    - Use whole stanzas?
    - Use the same structure and rhyme scheme?

STUDY OF A POET: INUA ELLAMS

Two Poems – 'Directions', by Billy Collins and 'Directions, after Billy Collins', by Inua Ellams

Inua Ellams' poem 'Directions' follows the structure, language and content of Billy Collins' poem, also called 'Directions', very closely. This is not a coincidence. Ellams does this deliberately to create a particular effect, and acknowledges the link in his sub-heading 'after Billy Collins'. You are going to look at both poems side-by-side in order to think more closely about poets borrowing from other poets.

- Listen to your teacher reading 'Directions' by Billy Collins on page 160-161.

- Turn to the person next to you and share your first thoughts about the poem, for example anything that especially interests you or anything that puzzles you about it.

- Either listen to Inua Ellams introduce and read 'Directions' or listen as your teacher reads it. You can follow along on page 162-163.

- Turn to the person next to you and share your first thoughts about this poem, for example anything that interests or puzzles you about it and the connections it has with the Billy Collins' poem that you previously read.

On page 164 there are more activities to help you investigate the links between the poems more fully.

Directions

You know the brick path in back of the house,
the one you see from the kitchen window,
the one that bends around the far end of the garden
where all the yellow primroses are?
And you know how if you leave the path
and walk up into the woods you come
to a heap of rocks, probably pushed
down during the horrors of the Ice Age,
and a grove of tall hemlocks, dark green now
against the light-brown fallen leaves?
And farther on, you know
the small footbridge with the broken railing
and if you go beyond that you arrive
at the bottom of that sheep's head hill?
Well, if you start climbing, and you
might have to grab hold of a sapling
when the going gets steep,
you will eventually come to a long stone
ridge with a border of pine trees
which is as high as you can go
and a good enough place to stop.

The best time is late afternoon
when the sun strobes through
the columns of trees as you are hiking up,
and when you find an agreeable rock
to sit on, you will be able to see
the light pouring down into the woods
and breaking into the shapes and tones
of things and you will hear nothing
but a sprig of birdsong or the leafy

STUDY OF A POET – INUA ELLAMS

falling of a cone or nut through the trees,
and if this is your day you might even
spot a hare or feel the wing-beats of geese
driving overhead toward some destination.

But it is hard to speak of these things
how the voices of light enter the body
and begin to recite their stories
how the earth holds us painfully against
its breast made of humus and brambles
how we who will soon be gone regard
the entities that continue to return
greener than ever, spring water flowing
through a meadow and the shadows of clouds
passing over the hills and the ground
where we stand in the tremble of thought
taking the vast outside into ourselves.

Still, let me know before you set out.
Come knock on my door
and I will walk with you as far as the garden
with one hand on your shoulder.
I will even watch after you and not turn back
to the house until you disappear
into the crowd of maple and ash,
heading up toward the hill,
piercing the ground with your stick

Billy Collins

Directions

– after Billy Collins

You know the wild bush at the back of the flat,
the one that scrapes the kitchen window,
the one that struggles for soil and water
and fails where the train tracks scar the ground?
And you know how if you leave the bush
and walk the stunted land, you come
to crossroads, paved just weeks ago:
hot tar over the flattened roots of trees,
and a squad of traffic lights, red-eyed now
stiff against the filth-stained fallen leaves?

And farther on, you know
the bruised allotments with the broken sheds
and if you go beyond that you hit
the first block of Thomas Street Estate?
Well, if you enter and ascend, and you
might need a running jump over
dank puddles into the shaking lift
that goes no further than the fourth floor,
you will eventually come to a rough rise
of stairs that reach without railings
the run-down roof as high as you can go
and a good place to stop.

The best time is late evening
when the moon fights through
drifts of fumes as you are walking,
and when you find an upturned bin
to sit on, you will be able to see
the smog pour across the city

STUDY OF A POET – INUA ELLAMS

and blur the shapes and tones
of things and you will be attacked
by the symphony of tires, airplanes,
sirens, screams, engines –
and if this is your day you might even
catch a car chase or a hear a horde
of biker boys thunder-cross a bridge.

But it is tough to speak these things
how tufts of smog enter the body
and begin to wind us down,
how the city chokes us painfully against
its chest made of secrets and fire,
how we, built of weaker things, regard
our sculpted landscape, water flowing
through pipes, the clicks of satellites
passing over clouds and the roofs
where we stand in the shudder of progress
giving ourselves to the vast outsides.

Still, text me before you set out.
Knock when you reach my door
and I will walk you as far as the tracks
with water for your travels and a hug.
I will watch after you and not turn back
to the flat till you merge
with the throngs of buses and cyclists –
heading down toward the block,
scuffing the ground with your feet.

Inua Ellams

KS3 POETRY PLUS

'Directions', the Remix

- Working in a group of three or four, investigate the two poems using the headings, below. Prepare to feed back to the whole class on the aspect of the poem you have been looking at particularly closely.

- Share your thinking as a class and discuss what you like about the way Ellams has remixed 'Directions'.

Phrases or lines

Find phrases or lines that are used in both poems. How are they used in similar or different ways?

The setting

Look at similarities and differences in the setting, including the time of day, the season and where the poem takes place.

The speaker

Billy Collins uses a first person speaker who directly addresses someone as 'you'. We don't know exactly who he is speaking to but the repetition of 'you know' and the image of him watching over the person as they leave makes it sound as if he is speaking to a friend who shares some knowledge of the place. Look at similarities and differences in the speaker of Ellams' poem.

The structure

Billy Collins writes with no regular rhythm or rhyme but all his lines are about the same length. His sentences run on over several lines, apart from the first line in the last stanza: 'Still, let me know before you set out.' Investigate similarities and differences in the structure of Ellams' poem.

Themes

Billy Collins begins with a description of walking a path, but his poem takes a turn when he writes 'But it is hard to speak of these things'. He talks about how everything that lives will die, but also the way nature will renew in spring 'greener than ever'. What does Ellams seem to be discussing when he writes 'But it is tough to speak these things…'?

STUDY OF A POET – INUA ELLAMS

Over to You – Your Own 'Directions'

You are going to create your own poem titled 'Directions', using a setting that you know well and borrowing ideas from both Ellams and Collins.

1. Creating a setting

- Working individually, choose a setting you know well and decide on a time of day and a time of year.

- Sit back-to-back with a partner. One person should close their eyes while the other person gives them a 'virtual tour' of their chosen setting. If you are the describer, try to make your description as vivid as possible and include as much sensory information as you can, for example what you can hear or touch. If you are the listener, listen out for particularly good bits of description which could be used in a piece of writing.

- When the describer has finished, discuss which bits of your description would work well in a poem. Work together to make notes to help you to remember these for when you start writing.

- Swap roles and repeat the activity.

2. Stealing ideas

- Working individually, re-read both Inua Ellams' poem and Billy Collins' poem. Make a note of anything you would like to borrow for your own poem, for example:
  - The structure
  - Particular words or phrases
  - Themes
  - The way the speaker addresses the friend.

3. A first draft

Working on your own, draw on your notes to write a first draft of your poem, working fairly quickly to get your ideas on paper but not worrying about it too much at this stage.

KS3 POETRY PLUS

4. Reflecting on the decisions poets make

In a poem, every word should earn its keep. The images, the order of the words and the decisions the poet makes about where to end one line and begin the next all help to create the poem's meaning.

▌ Before re-drafting your poem, use the prompts below to help you think critically about some of the decisions Ellams and Collins took when writing their poems.

Similes or metaphors
▌ Do similes or metaphors work best in a particular line? For example, think about why Ellams wrote:

> how the city chokes us painfully against
> its chest made of secrets and fire,

rather than

> It is as if the city chokes us painfully against
> its chest made of secrets and fire,

Line endings
▌ Where should the line breaks go? Think, for instance, about the effect of Collins' decision to put particular words (shown here in bold) at the beginning or end of a line.

> …and you will **hear nothing**
> but a sprig of birdsong or the **leafy**
> **falling** of a cone or nut through the trees,

Word order
▌ Think about why Ellams writes:

> and a squad of traffic lights, red-eyed now

rather than

> And a squad of red-eyed traffic lights

5. A final draft

▌ Using what you have learned by looking closely at Ellams' and Collins' decisions, review your own poem with a critical eye. Think hard about:

- ▶ Your choice of images
- ▶ Word order
- ▶ Where you choose to end one line and begin another.

▌ Now write a final draft of your poem.

STUDY OF A POET – INUA ELLAMS

Author Study – On Reflection

- Working with a partner, choose two poems from this section to reflect more broadly on Ellams' style.

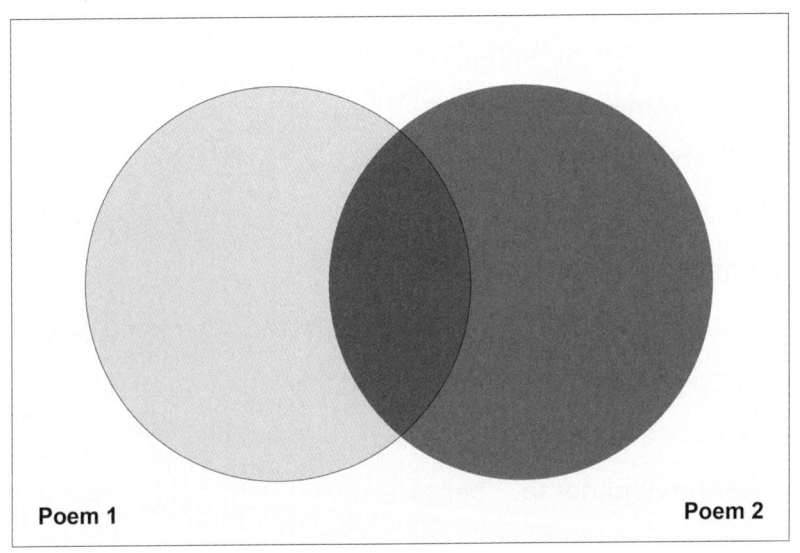

Poem 1 / Poem 2 (Venn diagram)

- With your partner, draw a Venn diagram like the one below.

- With your partner, discuss the features below and decide where to put them on your Venn diagram – in one circle if Ellams uses this feature in one poem only, in the overlap in the middle if this is something the poems have in common, outside the circles if you don't think this statement applies to either poem.

Features

A. Draws from personal experience

B. Talks about big, global issues

C. Seems to be addressing someone the speaker knows

D. Uses echoes and repetitions

E. Uses humour

F. Remixes

G. Has an urban setting

H. Uses imagery

I. Doesn't use regular rhythm or rhyme

J. Contains dialogue marked with slashes (/)

K. Influenced by his Nigerian experience and culture

L. More like prose

M. Contains lots of conventional poetic features

N. Uses everyday language

O. Tells a story

KS3 POETRY PLUS

▌ Working individually, draw on your discussion and your Venn diagram to write at least two paragraphs about similarities you have noticed in the two poems and at least one paragraph about a difference you have noticed in the two poems. You could use the prompts below to help you if you wish.

- Ellams often… and in Poem X and Y he…
- Ellams sometimes… but in poem X he…
- Poem X… but Poem Y…
- Poem X…. and Poem Y also…
- Both poems… I think this is because…
- I like the fact that poem X… because… On the other hand, poem Y is…
- Compared with poem X, poem Y… and this…
- Both poem X and poem Y… so…
- I think Ellams chooses to… because…
- I prefer poem X because it…

ANTHOLOGY OF POEMS

KS3 POETRY PLUS ANTHOLOGY

Beowulf (2 extracts)

Extract 1

Grendel this monster grim was called,
march-riever mighty, in moorland living,
in fen and fastness; fief of the giants
the hapless wight a while had kept
since the Creator his exile doomed.

Extract 2

Went he forth to find at fall of night
that haughty house, and heed wherever
the Ring-Danes, outrevelled, to rest had gone.
Found within it the atheling band
asleep after feasting and fearless of sorrow,
of human hardship. Unhallowed wight,
grim and greedy, he grasped betimes,
wrathful, reckless, from resting-places,
thirty of the thanes, and thence he rushed
fain of his fell spoil, faring homeward,
laden with slaughter, his lair to seek.
Then at the dawning, as day was breaking,
the might of Grendel to men was known;
then after wassail was wail uplifted,
loud moan in the morn. The mighty chief,
atheling excellent, unblithe sat,
laboured in woe for the loss of his thanes,
when once had been traced the trail of the fiend,
spirit accurst: too cruel that sorrow,
too long, too loathsome. Not late the respite;
with night returning, anew began
ruthless murder; he recked no whit,
firm in his guilt, of the feud and crime.

Anon, translated by Francis B. Grummere (c. 11th century)

Piers the Plowman

In a summer season · when soft was the sun,
I clothed myself in a cloak as I shepherd were,
Habit like a hermit's · unholy in works,
And went wide in the world · wonders to hear.
But on a May morning · on Malvern hills,
A marvel befell me · of fairy, methought.
I was weary with wandering · and went me to rest
Under a broad bank · by a brook's side,
And as I lay and leaned over · and looked into the waters
I fell into a sleep · for it sounded so merry.
Then began I to dream · a marvellous dream,
That I was in a wilderness · wist I not where.
As I looked to the east · right into the sun,
I saw a tower on a toft · worthily built;
A deep dale beneath · a dungeon therein,
With deep ditches and dark · and dreadful of sight
A fair field full of folk · found I in between,
Of all manner of men · the rich and the poor,
Working and wandering · as the world asketh.
Some put them to plow · and played little enough,
At setting and sowing · they sweated right hard
And won that which wasters · by gluttony destroy.

William Langland (late 14th century; modern translation)

I Find No Peace

I find no peace, and all my war is done.
I fear and hope. I burn and freeze like ice.
I fly above the wind, yet can I not arise;
And nought I have, and all the world I season.
That loseth nor locketh holdeth me in prison
And holdeth me not—yet can I scape no wise—
Nor letteth me live nor die at my device,
And yet of death it giveth me occasion.
Without eyen I see, and without tongue I plain.
I desire to perish, and yet I ask health.
I love another, and thus I hate myself.
I feed me in sorrow and laugh in all my pain;
Likewise displeaseth me both life and death,
And my delight is causer of this strife.

Sir Thomas Wyatt (1503-1542)

On Monsieur's Departure

I grieve and dare not show my discontent,
I love and yet am forced to seem to hate,
I do, yet dare not say I ever meant,
I seem stark mute but inwardly do prate.
   I am and not, I freeze and yet am burned,
   Since from myself my other self I turned.

My care is like my shadow in the sun,
Follows me flying, flies when I pursue it,
Stands and lies by me, doth what I have done.
His too familiar care doth make me rue it.
   No means I find to rid him from my breast,
   Till by the end of things it be supprest.

Some gentler passion slide into my mind,
For I am soft and made of melting snow;
Or be more cruel, love, and so be kind.
Let me or float or sink, be high or low.
   Or let me live with some more sweet content,
   Or die and so forget what love ere meant.

Queen Elizabeth I (1533-1603)

The Death of Queen Jane

Queen Jane lay in labour full nine days or more,
Till the women were so tired, they could stay no longer there,

'Good women, good women, good women as ye be,
Do open my right side and find my baby.'

'Oh no,' said the women. 'That never may be,
We will send for King Henry, and hear what he say.'

King Henry was sent for, King Henry did come:
'What do ail you, my lady, your eyes look so dim?'

'King Henry, King Henry, will you do one thing for me?
That's to open my right side, and find my baby.'

'Oh, no,' said King Henry. 'That's a thing I'll never do.
If I lose the flower of England, I shall lose the branch too.'

King Henry went mourning, and so did his men,
And so did the dear baby, for Queen Jane did die then.

And how deep was the mourning, how black were the bands,
How yellow, yellow were the flamboys they carried in their hands.

There was fiddling, aye, and dancing on the day the babe was born
But poor Queen Jane beloved lay cold as a stone.

A Folk Song (c. 1540, recorded 1907)

Sonnet 130

My mistress' eyes are nothing like the sun;
Coral is far more red than her lips' red;
If snow be white, why then her breasts are dun;
If hairs be wires, black wires grow on her head.
I have seen roses damasked, red and white,
But no such roses see I in her cheeks;
And in some perfumes is there more delight
Than in the breath that from my mistress reeks.
I love to hear her speak, yet well I know
That music hath a far more pleasing sound;
I grant I never saw a goddess go;
My mistress when she walks treads on the ground.
    And yet, by heaven, I think my love as rare
    As any she belied with false compare.

William Shakespeare (1564-1616)

On My First Sonne

Farewell, thou child of my right hand, and joy;
My sin was too much hope of thee, lov'd boy.
Seven years tho' wert lent to me, and I thee pay,
Exacted by thy fate, on the just day.
O, could I lose all father now! For why
Will man lament the state he should envy?
To have so soon 'scap'd world's and flesh's rage,
And if no other misery, yet age?
Rest in soft peace, and, ask'd, say, "Here doth lie
Ben Jonson his best piece of poetry."
For whose sake henceforth all his vows be such,
As what he loves may never like too much.

Ben Jonson (1572-1637)

A Song

Love, thou art best of Human Joys,
Our chiefest Happiness below;
All other Pleasures are but Toys,
Musick without Thee is but Noise,
And Beauty but an empty show.

Heav'n, who knew best what Man wou'd move,
And raise his Thoughts above the Brute;
Said, Let him Be, and Let him Love;
That must alone his Soul improve,
Howe'er Philosophers dispute.

Anne Finch, Countess of Winchelsea (1661-1720)

A Red, Red Rose

O my Luve is like a red, red rose
   That's newly sprung in June;
O my Luve is like the melody
   That's sweetly played in tune.

So fair art thou, my bonnie lass,
   So deep in luve am I;
And I will luve thee still, my dear,
   Till a' the seas gang dry.

Till a' the seas gang dry, my dear,
   And the rocks melt wi' the sun;
I will love thee still, my dear,
   While the sands o' life shall run.

And fare thee weel, my only luve!
   And fare thee weel awhile!
And I will come again, my luve,
   Though it were ten thousand mile.

Robert Burns (1759-1796)

The Schoolboy

I love to rise in a summer morn
When the birds sing on every tree;
The distant huntsman winds his horn,
And the skylark sings with me.
O! what sweet company.

But to go to school in a summer morn,
O! it drives all joy away;
Under a cruel eye outworn,
The little ones spend the day
In sighing and dismay.

Ah! then at times I drooping sit,
And spend many an anxious hour,
Nor in my book can I take delight,
Nor sit in learning's bower,
Worn thro' with the dreary shower.

How can the bird that is born for joy
Sit in a cage and sing?
How can a child, when fears annoy,
But droop his tender wing,
And forget his youthful spring?

O! father and mother, if buds are nipp'd
And blossoms blown away,
And if the tender plants are stripp'd
Of their joy in the springing day,
By sorrow and care's dismay,

How shall the summer arise in joy,
Or the summer fruits appear?
Or how shall we gather what griefs destroy,
Or bless the mellowing year,
When the blasts of winter appear?

William Blake (1757-1827)

ANTHOLOGY OF POEMS

Composed Upon Westminster Bridge

Earth has not anything to show more fair:
Dull would he be of soul who could pass by
A sight so touching in its majesty:
This City now doth, like a garment, wear
The beauty of the morning; silent, bare,
Ships, towers, domes, theatres, and temples lie
Open unto the fields, and to the sky;
All bright and glittering in the smokeless air.
Never did sun more beautifully steep
In his first splendour, valley, rock, or hill;
Ne'er saw I, never felt, a calm so deep!
The river glideth at his own sweet will:
Dear God! the very houses seem asleep;
And all that mighty heart is lying still!

William Wordsworth (1770-1850)

Limerick

There was an Old Man with a beard,
Who said, 'It is just as I feared!
Two Owls and a Hen,
Four Larks and a Wren,
Have all built their nests in my beard!'

Edward Lear (1812-1888)

The Rime of the Ancient Mariner (Extract)

And now the STORM-BLAST
              came, and he
Was tyrannous and strong:
He struck with his o'ertaking wings,
And chased us south along.

With sloping masts and dipping prow,
As who pursued with yell and blow
Still treads the shadow of his foe,
And forward bends his head,
The ship drove fast, loud roared the
              blast,
And southward aye we fled.

And now there came both mist and
              snow,
And it grew wondrous cold:
And ice, mast-high, came floating by,
As green as emerald.

And through the drifts the snowy clifts
Did send a dismal sheen:
Nor shapes of men nor beasts we ken—
The ice was all between.

The ice was here, the ice was there,
The ice was all around:
It cracked and growled, and roared and
              howled,
Like noises in a swound!

At length did cross an Albatross,
Thorough the fog it came;
As if it had been a Christian soul,
We hailed it in God's name.

It ate the food it ne'er had eat,
And round and round it flew.
The ice did split with a thunder-fit;
The helmsman steered us through!

And a good south wind sprung up
              behind;
The Albatross did follow,
And every day, for food or play,
Came to the mariner's hollo!

In mist or cloud, on mast or shroud,
It perched for vespers nine;
Whiles all the night, through fog
              smoke white,
Glimmered the white Moon-shine.'

'God save thee, ancient Mariner!
From the fiends, that plague thee
              thus!—
Why look'st thou so?'—With my
              cross-bow
I shot the ALBATROSS.

Samuel Taylor Coleridge (1772-1834)

No!

  No sun—no moon!
  No morn—no noon—
No dawn—
  No sky—no earthly view—
  No distance looking blue—
No road—no street—no "t'other side the way"—
  No end to any Row—
  No indications where the Crescents go—
  No top to any steeple—
No recognitions of familiar people—
  No courtesies for showing 'em—
  No knowing 'em!
No traveling at all—no locomotion,
No inkling of the way—no notion—
  "No go"—by land or ocean—
  No mail—no post—
  No news from any foreign coast—
No park—no ring—no afternoon gentility—
  No company—no nobility—
No warmth, no cheerfulness, no healthful ease,
 No comfortable feel in any member—
No shade, no shine, no butterflies, no bees,
No fruits, no flowers, no leaves, no birds,
  November!

Thomas Hood (1799-1845)

The Foddering Boy

The foddering boy along the crumping snows
With straw-band-belted legs and folded arm
Hastens, and on the blast that keenly blows
Oft turns for breath, and beats his fingers warm,
And shakes the lodging snows from off his clothes,
Buttoning his doublet closer from the storm
And slouching his brown beaver o'er his nose –
Then faces it agen, and seeks the stack
Within its circling fence where hungry lows
Expecting cattle, making many a track
About the snows, impatient for the sound
When in hugh forkfuls trailing at his back
He litters sweet hay about the ground
And brawls to call the staring cattle round.

John Clare (1793-1864)

The Night Is Darkening Round Me

The night is darkening round me,
The wild winds coldly blow;
But a tyrant spell has bound me,
And I cannot, cannot go.

The giant trees are bending
Their bare boughs weighed with snow;
The storm is fast descending,
And yet I cannot go.

Clouds beyond clouds above me,
Wastes beyond wastes below;
But nothing drear can move me;
I will not, cannot go.

Emily Brontë (1818-1848)

ANTHOLOGY OF POEMS

Fall, Leaves, Fall

Fall, leaves, fall; die, flowers, away;
Lengthen night and shorten day;
Every leaf speaks bliss to me
Fluttering from the autumn tree.
I shall smile when wreaths of snow
Blossom where the rose should grow;
I shall sing when night's decay
Ushers in a drearier day.

Emily Brontë (1818-1848)

The Shortest and Sweetest of Songs

Come
Home.

George MacDonald (1824-1905)

Sonnets From the Portuguese 43: How Do I Love Thee?

How do I love thee? Let me count the ways.
I love thee to the depth and breadth and height
My soul can reach, when feeling out of sight
For the ends of being and ideal grace.
I love thee to the level of every day's
Most quiet need, by sun and candle-light.
I love thee freely, as men strive for right;
I love thee purely, as they turn from praise.
I love thee with the passion put to use
In my old griefs, and with my childhood's faith.
I love thee with a love I seemed to lose
With my lost saints. I love thee with the breath,
Smiles, tears, of all my life; and, if God choose,
I shall but love thee better after death.

Elizabeth Barrett Browning (1806-1861)

632

The Brain—is wider than the Sky—
For—put them side by side—
The one the other will contain
With ease—and You—beside—

The Brain is deeper than the sea—
For—hold them—Blue to Blue—
The one the other will absorb—
As Sponges—Buckets—do—

The Brain is just the weight of God—
For—Heft them—Pound for Pound—
And they will differ—if they do—
As Syllable from Sound—

Emily Dickinson (1830-1886)

Pied Beauty

Glory be to God for dappled things –
   For skies of couple-colour as a brinded cow;
      For rose-moles all in stipple upon trout that swim;
Fresh-firecoal chestnut-falls; finches' wings;
   Landscape plotted and pieced – fold, fallow, and plough;
     And áll trádes, their gear and tackle and trim.

All things counter, original, spare, strange;
   Whatever is fickle, freckled (who knows how?)
     With swift, slow; sweet, sour; adazzle, dim;
He fathers-forth whose beauty is past change:
        Praise him.

Gerard Manley Hopkins (1844-1899)

ANTHOLOGY OF POEMS

The Eagle

He clasps the crag with crooked hands;
Close to the sun in lonely lands,
Ring'd with the azure world, he stands.

The wrinkled sea beneath him crawls;
He watches from his mountain walls,
And like a thunderbolt he falls.

Alfred, Lord Tennyson (1809-1892)

Up-hill

Does the road wind up-hill all the way?
   Yes, to the very end.
Will the day's journey take the whole long day?
   From morn to night, my friend.

But is there for the night a resting-place?
   A roof for when the slow dark hours begin.
May not the darkness hide it from my face?
   You cannot miss that inn.

Shall I meet other wayfarers at night?
   Those who have gone before.
Then must I knock, or call when just in sight?
   They will not keep you standing at that door.

Shall I find comfort, travel-sore and weak?
   Of labour you shall find the sum.
Will there be beds for me and all who seek?
   Yea, beds for all who come.

Christina Rossetti (1830-1894)

I Hear America Singing

I hear America singing, the varied carols I hear,
Those of mechanics, each one singing his as it should be blithe and strong,
The carpenter singing his as he measures his plank or beam,
The mason singing his as he makes ready for work, or leaves off work,
The boatman singing what belongs to him in his boat, the deckhand singing on the steamboat deck,
The shoemaker singing as he sits on his bench, the hatter singing as he stands,
The wood-cutter's song, the ploughboy's on his way in the morning, or at noon intermission or at sundown,
The delicious singing of the mother, or of the young wife at work, or of the girl sewing or washing,
Each singing what belongs to him or her and to none else,
The day what belongs to the day—at night the party of young fellows, robust, friendly,
Singing with open mouths their strong melodious songs.

Walt Whitman (1819-1892)

He Wishes For the Cloths of Heaven

Had I the heavens' embroidered cloths,
Enwrought with golden and silver light,
The blue and the dim and the dark cloths
Of night and light and the half-light,
I would spread the cloths under your feet:
But I, being poor, have only my dreams;
I have spread my dreams under your feet;
Tread softly because you tread on my dreams.

W.B. Yeats (1865-1939)

Invitation to Love

Come when the nights are bright with stars
Or come when the moon is mellow;
Come when the sun his golden bars
Drops on the hay-field yellow.
Come in the twilight soft and gray,
Come in the night or come in the day,
Come, O love, whene'er you may,
And you are welcome, welcome.

You are sweet, O Love, dear Love,
You are soft as the nesting dove.
Come to my heart and bring it to rest
As the bird flies home to its welcome nest.

Come when my heart is full of grief
Or when my heart is merry;
Come with the falling of the leaf
Or with the redd'ning cherry.
Come when the year's first blossom blows,
Come when the summer gleams and glows,
Come with the winter's drifting snows,
And you are welcome, welcome.

Paul Lawrence Dunbar (1872-1906)

Cork and Work and Card and Ward

I take it you already know
Of tough and bough and cough and dough?
Others may stumble, but not you
On hiccough, thorough, laugh, and through?
I write in case you wish perhaps
To learn of less familiar traps:
Beware of heard, a dreadful word
That looks like beard, and sounds like bird.
And dead: it's said like bed, not bead;
For goodness' sake, don't call it 'deed'!
Watch out for meat and great and threat
(They rhyme with suite and straight and debt).
A moth is not a moth in mother,
Nor both in bother, broth in brother.
And here is not a match for there,
Nor dear for bear, or fear for pear.
There's dose and rose, there's also lose
(Just look them up), and goose, and choose,
And cork and work, and card and ward,
And font and front, and word and sword,
And do and go and thwart and cart –
Come come, I've barely made a start!
A dreadful language? Man alive,
I'd mastered it when I was five!

Anon (c. 1900)

Old houses were scaffolding once
                        and workmen whistling.

T.E. Hulme (1883-1917)

ANTHOLOGY OF POEMS

Autumn

A touch of cold in the Autumn night—
I walked abroad,
And saw the ruddy moon lean over a hedge
Like a red-faced farmer.
I did not stop to speak, but nodded,
And round about were the wistful stars
With white faces like town children.

T.E. Hulme (1883-1917)

Rain

Rain, midnight rain, nothing but the wild rain
On this bleak hut, and solitude, and me
Remembering again that I shall die
And neither hear the rain nor give it thanks
For washing me cleaner than I have been
Since I was born into solitude.
Blessed are the dead that the rain rains upon:
But here I pray that none whom once I loved
Is dying tonight or lying still awake
Solitary, listening to the rain,
Either in pain or thus in sympathy
Helpless among the living and the dead,
Like a cold water among broken reeds,
Myriads of broken reeds all still and stiff,
Like me who have no love which this wild rain
Has not dissolved except the love of death,
If love it be towards what is perfect and
Cannot, the tempest tells me, disappoint.

Edward Thomas (1883-1917)

Night Song at Amalfi

I asked the heaven of stars
   What I should give my love —
It answered me with silence,
   Silence above.

I asked the darkened sea
   Down where the fishes go —
It answered me with silence,
   Silence below.

Oh, I could give him weeping,
   Or I could give him song —
But how can I give silence
   My whole life long?

Sara Teasdale (1884-1933)

Dust of Snow

The way a crow
Shook down on me
The dust of snow
From a hemlock tree

Has given my heart
A change of mood
And saved some part
Of a day I had rued.

Robert Frost (1874-1963)

The Road Not Taken

Two roads diverged in a yellow wood,
And sorry I could not travel both
And be one traveler, long I stood
And looked down one as far as I could
To where it bent in the undergrowth;

Then took the other, as just as fair,
And having perhaps the better claim,
Because it was grassy and wanted wear;
Though as for that, the passing there
Had worn them really about the same,

And both that morning equally lay
In leaves no step had trodden black.
Oh, I kept the first for another day!
Yet knowing how way leads on to way,
I doubted if I should ever come back.

I shall be telling this with a sigh
Somewhere ages and ages hence:
Two roads diverged in a wood, and I—
I took the one less traveled by,
And that has made all the difference.

Robert Frost (1874-1963)

Nothing Gold Can Stay

Nature's first green is gold,
Her hardest hue to hold.
Her early leaf's a flower;
But only so an hour.
Then leaf subsides to leaf.
So Eden sank to grief,
So dawn goes down to day.
Nothing gold can stay.

Robert Frost (1874-1963)

Acquainted With the Night

I have been one acquainted with the night.
I have walked out in rain—and back in rain.
I have outwalked the furthest city light.

I have looked down the saddest city lane.
I have passed by the watchman on his beat
And dropped my eyes, unwilling to explain.

I have stood still and stopped the sound of feet
When far away an interrupted cry
Came over houses from another street,

But not to call me back or say good-by;
And further still at an unearthly height
One luminary clock against the sky

Proclaimed the time was neither wrong nor right.
I have been one acquainted with the night.

Robert Frost (1874-1963)

The Way Through the Woods

They shut the road through the woods
Seventy years ago.
Weather and rain have undone it again,
And now you would never know
There was once a road through the woods
Before they planted the trees.
It is underneath the coppice and heath,
And the thin anemones.
Only the keeper sees
That, where the ring-dove broods,
And the badgers roll at ease,
There was once a road through the woods.

Yet, if you enter the woods
Of a summer evening late,
When the night-air cools on the trout-ringed pools
Where the otter whistles his mate,
(They fear not men in the woods,
Because they see so few.)
You will hear the beat of a horse's feet,
And the swish of a skirt in the dew,
Steadily cantering through
The misty solitudes,
As though they perfectly knew
The old lost road through the woods.
But there is no road through the woods.

Rudyard Kipling (1865-1936)

Futility

Move him into the sun –
Gently its touch awoke him once,
At home, whispering of fields unsown.
Always it woke him, even in France,
Until this morning and this snow.
If anything might rouse him now
The kind old sun will know.

Think how it wakes the seeds, –
Woke, once, the clays of a cold star.
Are limbs, so dear-achieved, are sides
Full-nerved, – still warm, – too hard to stir?
Was it for this the clay grew tall?
– O what made fatuous sunbeams toil
To break earth's sleep at all?

Wilfred Owen (1893-1918)

ANTHOLOGY OF POEMS

Butterfly

Butterfly, the wind blows seaward, strong beyond the garden wall!
Butterfly, why do you settle on my shoe, and sip the dirt on my shoe,
Lifting your veined wings, lifting them? big white butterfly!

Already it is October, and the wind blows strong to the sea
from the hills where snow must have fallen, the wind is polished
    with snow.
Here in the garden, with red geraniums, it is warm, it is warm
but the wind blows strong to seaward, white butterfly, content on
    my shoe!

Will you go, will you go from my warm house?
Will you climb on your big soft wings, black-dotted,
as up an invisible rainbow, an arch
till the wind slides you sheer from the arch-crest
and in a strange level fluttering you go out to seaward, white speck!

Farewell, farewell, lost soul!
you have melted in the crystalline distance,
it is enough! I saw you vanish into air.

D.H. Lawrence (1914-1930)

Ye Cannae Shove Yer Granny Aff a Bus!

Ye cannae shove yer granny aff a bus,
Oh ye cannae shove yer granny aff a bus,
Ye cannae shove yer granny, for she's yer mammy's mammy,
Ye cannae shove yer granny aff a bus.

Ye can shove yer other granny aff a bus,
Ye can shove yer other granny aff a bus.
You can shove yer other granny, for she's yer daddy's mammy,
Ye can shove yer other granny aff a bus.

Anon (c. 20th century)

KS3 POETRY PLUS

Song From the Kitlinuharmiut (Copper Eskimo)

And I think over again
My small adventures
When from a shore wind I drifted out
In my kayak
And I thought I was in danger.

My fears,
Those small ones
That I thought so big,
For all the vital things
I had to get and to reach.

And yet, there is only
One great thing,
The only thing.
To live and see in huts and on journeys
The great day that dawns,
And the light that fills the world.

Anon (recorded c. 1920s)

John Bun

Here lies John Bun,
He was killed by a gun,
His name was not Bun, it was Wood,
But Wood would not rhyme with gun, but
                        Bun would.

Anon (c. 20th century)

ANTHOLOGY OF POEMS

[To Margot Heinemann]

Heart of the heartless world,
Dear heart, the thought of you
Is the pain at my side,
The shadow that chills my view.

The wind rises in the evening,
Reminds that autumn's near.
I am afraid to lose you,
I am afraid of my fear.

On the last mile to Huesca,
The last fence for our pride,
Think so kindly, dear, that I
Sense you at my side.

And if bad luck should lay my strength
Into the shallow grave,
Remember all the good you can;
Don't forget my love.

John Cornford (1915-1936)

Harlem [2]

What happens to a dream deferred?

    Does it dry up
    like a raisin in the sun?
    Or fester like a sore—
    And then run?
    Does it stink like rotten meat?
    Or crust and sugar over—
    like a syrupy sweet?

    Maybe it just sags
    like a heavy load.

Or does it explode?

Langston Hughes (1902-1967)

Time Does Not Bring Relief

Time does not bring relief; you all have lied
Who told me time would ease me of my pain!
I miss him in the weeping of the rain;
I want him at the shrinking of the tide;
The old snows melt from every mountain-side,
And last year's leaves are smoke in every lane;
But last year's bitter loving must remain
Heaped on my heart, and my old thoughts abide.
There are a hundred places where I fear
To go,—so with his memory they brim.
And entering with relief some quiet place
Where never fell his foot or shone his face
I say, 'There is no memory of him here!'
And so stand stricken, so remembering him.

Edna St Vincent Millay (1892-1950)

The Loch Ness Monster's Song

Sssnnnwhuffffll?
Hnwhuffl hhnnwfl hnfl hfl?
Gdroblboblhobngbl gbl gl g g g g glbgl.
Drublhaflablhaflubhafgabhaflhafl fl fl –
gm grawwwww grf grawf awfgm graw gm.
Hovoplodok – doplodovok – plovodokot-doplodokosh?
Splgraw fok fok splgrafhatchgabrlgabrl fok splfok!
Zgra kra gka fok!
Grof grawff gahf?
Gombl mbl bl –
blm plm,
blm plm,
blm plm,
blp.

Edwin Morgan (1920-2010)

ANTHOLOGY OF POEMS

Poem

Lana Turner has collapsed!
I was trotting along and suddenly
it started raining and snowing
and you said it was hailing
but hailing hits you on the head
hard so it was really snowing and
raining and I was in such a hurry
to meet you but the traffic
was exactly like the sky
and suddenly I see a headline
LANA TURNER HAS COLLAPSED!
there is no snow in Hollywood
there is no rain in California
I have been to lots of parties
and acted perfectly disgraceful
but I never actually collapsed
oh Lana Turner we love you get up

Frank O'Hara (1926-1966)

Animals

Have you forgotten what we were like then
when we were still first rate
and the day came fat with an apple in its mouth

it's no use worrying about Time
but we did have a few tricks up our sleeves
and turned some sharp corners

the whole pasture looked like our meal
we didn't need speedometers
we could manage cocktails out of ice and water

I wouldn't want to be faster
or greener than now if you were with me O you
were the best of all my days

Frank O'Hara (1926-1966)

Haiku Moments 1

1.
Full church is in song
for Jesus, born on this date:
holy – this arrest!

2.
Stems and leaves downy
hidden here white under stone –
to be green sunlight.

3.
Mango – you sucked from
sunrise to sunset to be
this ripe scented flesh.

4.
Settled in the bowl
alone, banana lies
there cuddle-curved, waiting.

5.
Fife-man, fife-man, O
yu flutin dance in mi head
see, me walk with it!

6.
Children out of school:
listen – those high voices on
thin and tubby legs.

James Berry (1924-2017)

Maighdean Mara

For Séan Oh-Eocha

I

She sleeps now, her cold breasts
Dandled by undertow,
Her hair lifted and laid.
Undulant slow seawracks
Cast about shin and thigh,
Bangles of wort, drifting
Liens catch, dislodge gently.

This is the great first sleep
Of homecoming, eight
Land years between hearth and
Bed, steeped and dishevelled.
Her magic garment al-
most ocean-tinctured still.

II

He stole her garment as
She combed her hair: follow
Was all that she could do.
He hid it in the eaves
And charmed her there, four walls,
Warm floor, man-love nightly
In earshot of the waves.

She suffered milk and birth—
She had no choice—conjured
Patterns of home and drained
The tidesong from her voice
Then the thatcher came and stuck
Her garment in a stack.
Children carried tales back.

III

In night air, entering
Foam, she wrapped herself
With smoke-reeks from his thatch,
Straw-musts and films of mildew.
She dipped his secret there
Forever and uncharmed

Accents of fisher wives,
The dead hold of bedrooms,
Dread of the night and morrow,
Her children's brush and combs.
She sleeps now, her cold breasts
Dandled by undertow.

Seamus Heaney (1939-2013)

Still I Rise

You may write me down in history
With your bitter, twisted lies,
You may trod me in the very dirt
But still, like dust, I'll rise.

Does my sassiness upset you?
Why are you beset with gloom?
'Cause I walk like I've got oil wells
Pumping in my living room.

Just like moons and like suns,
With the certainty of tides,
Just like hopes springing high,
Still I'll rise.

Did you want to see me broken?
Bowed head and lowered eyes?
Shoulders falling down like teardrops.
Weakened by my soulful cries?

Does my haughtiness offend you?
Don't you take it awful hard
'Cause I laugh like I've got gold mines
Diggin' in my own backyard.

You may shoot me with your words,
You may cut me with your eyes,
You may kill me with your hatefulness,
But still, like air, I'll rise.

Does my sexiness upset you?
Does it come as a surprise
That I dance like I've got diamonds
At the meeting of my thighs?

Out of the huts of history's shame
I rise
Up from a past that's rooted in pain
I rise
I'm a black ocean, leaping and wide,
Welling and swelling I bear in the tide.

Leaving behind nights of terror and fear
I rise
Into a daybreak that's wondrously clear
I rise
Bringing the gifts that my ancestors gave,
I am the dream and the hope of the slave.
I rise
I rise
I rise.

Maya Angelou (1928-2014)

Directions

You know the brick path in back of the house,
the one you see from the kitchen window,
the one that bends around the far end of the garden
where all the yellow primroses are?
And you know how if you leave the path
and walk up into the woods you come
to a heap of rocks, probably pushed
down during the horrors of the Ice Age,
and a grove of tall hemlocks, dark green now
against the light-brown fallen leaves?
And farther on, you know
the small footbridge with the broken railing
and if you go beyond that you arrive
at the bottom of that sheep's head hill?
Well, if you start climbing, and you
might have to grab hold of a sapling
when the going gets steep,
you will eventually come to a long stone
ridge with a border of pine trees
which is as high as you can go
and a good enough place to stop.

The best time is late afternoon
when the sun strobes through
the columns of trees as you are hiking up,
and when you find an agreeable rock
to sit on, you will be able to see
the light pouring down into the woods
and breaking into the shapes and tones
of things and you will hear nothing
but a sprig of birdsong or the leafy
falling of a cone or nut through the trees,
and if this is your day you might even

spot a hare or feel the wing-beats of geese
driving overhead toward some destination.

But it is hard to speak of these things
how the voices of light enter the body
and begin to recite their stories
how the earth holds us painfully against
its breast made of humus and brambles
how we who will soon be gone regard
the entities that continue to return
greener than ever, spring water flowing
through a meadow and the shadows of clouds
passing over the hills and the ground
where we stand in the tremble of thought
taking the vast outside into ourselves.

Still, let me know before you set out.
Come knock on my door
and I will walk with you as far as the garden
with one hand on your shoulder.
I will even watch after you and not turn back
to the house until you disappear
into the crowd of maple and ash,
heading up toward the hill,
piercing the ground with your stick

Billy Collins (1941-)

As I Go

My pot is an old paint container
I do not know
who bought it
I do not know
whose house it decorated
I picked the empty tin
in Cemetery Lane.
My lamp, a paraffin lamp
is an empty 280 ml bottle
labelled 40 per cent alcohol
I picked up the bottle in a trash bin.
My cup
is an old jam tin
I do not know who enjoyed the sweetness
I found the tin
in a storm-water drain.
My plate is a motor car hub-cap cover
I do not know
whose car it belonged to.
I found a boy wheeling it, playing with it.
My house is built
from plastic over cardboard
I found the plastic being blown by the wind
It's simple
I pick up my life
as I go.

Julius Chingono (1946-2011)

from No Assistance

without any assistance or guidance from you
i have loved you assiduously for 8 months 2 wks & a day
i have been stood up four times
i've left 7 packages on yr doorstep
forty poems 2 plants & 3 handmade notecards i left
town so i cd send to you have been no help to me
on my job
you call at 3:00 in the mornin on weekdays
so i cd drive 27½ miles cross the bay before i go to work
charmin charmin
but you are of no assistance
i want you to know
this waz an experiment
to see how selfish i cd be
if i wd really carry on to snare a possible lover
if i waz capable of debasin my self for the love of another
if i cd stand not being wanted
when i wanted to be wanted
& i cannot
so
with no further assistance & no guidance from you
i am endin this affair

this note is attached to a plant
i've been waterin since the day i met you
you may water it
yr damn self

Ntozake Shange (1948-)

Sonnet
(inspired by Sonnet 22)

My glass can't quite persuade me I am old –
In that respect my ageing eyes are kind –
But when I see a photograph, I'm told
The dismal truth: I've left my youth behind.
And when I try to get up from a chair
My knees remind me they are past their best.
The burden they have carried everywhere
Is heavier now. No wonder they protest.
Arthritic fingers, problematic neck,
Sometimes causing mild to moderate pain,
Could well persuade me I'm an ancient wreck
But here's what helps me to feel young again:
   My love, who fell for me so long ago,
   Still loves me just as much, and tells me so.

Wendy Cope (1945-)

Hijab Scene #7

No, I'm not bald under the scarf
No, I'm not from that country
where women can't drive cars
No, I would not like to defect
I'm already American
But thank you for offering
What else do you need to know
relevant to my buying insurance,
opening a bank account,
reserving a seat on a flight?
Yes, I speak English
Yes, I carry explosives
They're called words
And if you don't get up
Off your assumptions,
They're going to blow you away

Mohja Kahf (1967-)

ANTHOLOGY OF POEMS

Poem #907 Miss Charlotte Brown, Librarian, Goes Mad

Today, I have decided
to read every poem ever written
in the short history of our civilization.
I know it is a selfish thing

to read. Every poem ever written
has its good intentions. I know,
I know, it is a selfish thing.
I want to believe that. Poetry

has its good intentions. I know
reading poems can't help much.
I want to believe that poetry
books have the answer. I'll start

reading. Poems can't help much
in the short history of our civilization.
Books have the answer. I'll start
today. I have decided.

Felix Jung (c. 1970s-)

Trainers All Turn Grey

(after Robert Frost's 'Nothing Gold Can Stay)

You buy your trainers new.
They cost a bob or two.
At first they're clean and white,
The laces thick and tight.
Then they must touch the ground –
(You have to walk around).
You learn to your dismay
Trainers all turn grey.

Sophie Hannah (1971-)

Directions
– after Billy Collins

You know the wild bush at the back of the flat,
the one that scrapes the kitchen window,
the one that struggles for soil and water
and fails where the train tracks scar the ground?
And you know how if you leave the bush
and walk the stunted land, you come
to crossroads, paved just weeks ago:
hot tar over the flattened roots of trees,
and a squad of traffic lights, red-eyed now
stiff against the filth-stained fallen leaves?

And farther on, you know
the bruised allotments with the broken sheds
and if you go beyond that you hit
the first block of Thomas Street Estate?
Well, if you enter and ascend, and you
might need a running jump over
dank puddles into the shaking lift
that goes no further than the fourth floor,
you will eventually come to a rough rise
of stairs that reach without railings
the run-down roof as high as you can go
and a good place to stop.

The best time is late evening
when the moon fights through
drifts of fumes as you are walking,
and when you find an upturned bin
to sit on, you will be able to see
the smog pour across the city
and blur the shapes and tones

of things and you will be attacked
by the symphony of tires, airplanes,
sirens, screams, engines –
and if this is your day you might even
catch a car chase or a hear a horde
of biker boys thunder-cross a bridge.

But it is tough to speak these things
how tufts of smog enter the body
and begin to wind us down,
how the city chokes us painfully against
its chest made of secrets and fire,
how we, built of weaker things, regard
our sculpted landscape, water flowing
through pipes, the clicks of satellites
passing over clouds and the roofs
where we stand in the shudder of progress
giving ourselves to the vast outsides.

Still, text me before you set out.
Knock when you reach my door
and I will walk you as far as the tracks
with water for your travels and a hug.
I will watch after you and not turn back
to the flat till you merge
with the throngs of buses and cyclists –
heading down toward the block,
scuffing the ground with your feet.

Inua Ellams (1984-)

Summit of Flight

Mother means well. She is in the next room
but knows I'm crushing socks into balls
of white cotton and shoving them down
the throat of my sneakers as she shouts
/ Are you off to play that game again? /

When I don't answer but squeeze and roll
my old towel till it's silent and forlorn
like a dead body I lift into the black bag,
she wants to know / Why not football
like everybody else. /

Mother means well but I wring the neck
of my water bottle when she yells
/ Even rugby is better than throwing
a large onion into a basket like a girl
in a market, it's a game for girls /

she says as I twist two sweat bands
like wrists into my back pocket
/ Sailing, cycling, anything else, but
you had to pick what no one cares
about, what kind of kid does that? /

Mother means well, as I shoulder the bag
and stare down the summit of flight
of stairs imagining the many routes out
of the house, each one a multitude
of lines and circles – perfect geometry

on which to forge my path. I stay low,
five strides and I've passed each creak
and crevice, pivoted on the last step,
edged the sharp desk onto the carpet,
nimbling towards the door

without a sound or uttered word,
only the human breath pushed down
the tangled line of tendon, muscle, bone
and the human spirit's strive to lift it all,
all the while spinning the ball like a world,

a lone star on a fingertip, out on a limb,
brighter for all the empty darkness around it,
floating through the door. Before it slams
Mother asks why I play the game. I respond
softly / You just won't understand /

Inua Ellams (1984-)

Ghetto van Gogh

The night my mother tells the story of the thief I am cross-legged on her lap. Her mouth is inches from my ear. She lets the dusk slip into her voice and whispers about the boy who snatched a mango at the market and ran, becoming the teenager who robbed a shop at gun point, shot the blind cashier, shot him as he fell, shot him once more dead; became the man who stole 36 cars and when apprehended, to be publicly hanged, asked for one wish, his whole lip quivering.

My mother who is inches from my ear, explains his dying wish to speak to his mother. The crowd parted silently, she gathered his bound wrists, kissed his rough skin, her cheeks shimmering in the killing heat. He bent forward, says mother, her mouth even closer, dusky voice hushed, bent towards her cheek as if to kiss goodbye and switched sharply, bit into her ear, strained against the flesh, ripped the thing off and spat / you should have told me mother, what I did was wrong /.

Inua Ellams (1984-)

Dear Tina

The day I discovered how she survived the civil war,
how she saw her friends pass like minutes into oblivion,
how she screamed through drop zones and Morse codes
into jungle, dodging bullets, hiding and crying into rain,

the day I discovered my grandfather heard her wailing,
felt something enough to move him after her, in darkness,
through rain, how her eyes, found in the flickering bounce
of hurricane lamps, showed a place so pure, he sailed her

away to the embrace of Paris, the kiss of Rome, the world
with its wide welcoming dome. The day I discovered this,
why she called him hero, she died. Peacefully, 90 years old.
He followed an hour after, again into darkness.

All those years, he never let go. That day, I realised we live
in different worlds; friends pass too fast for minutes, wars
come after X Factor, turtle dove romances exist in the past.

But I will send one sentence to you. One text message
screaming through wifi zones, digital codes, dodging
ones and zeros, like bullets and anti-heroes, promising

if evr ur lst n ths urbn jngle,
i'll fnd n brng u in frm rain.

Inua Ellams (1984-)

The Weight

I remember the first time I held a gun;
my cousin told me not to touch it.
It was an evil and malicious thing;
dark brown and the sun bounced off it
like oiled skin at the beach,
polished into a blazing sun.
It was heavy.
I dared myself to move. I'd seen its bullets before.

They looked like hand-held coffins;
the gold tips, a silk-lined open casket.

I tried to pick up the Kalashnikov.
It was something new; I was not afraid
but I wasn't strong enough to carry it.
It was heavy,
weighted down by
all those people's lives taken,
all those futures now gone for good.

I hear their whispers and cries haunting me,
feel the air thicken,
feel the world evaporating around me.
Silence screams at me.

Maryam Hussein (21st century)

Refugees

They have no need of our help
So do not tell me
These haggard faces could belong to you or me
Should life have dealt a different hand
We need to see them for who they really are
Chancers and scroungers
Layabouts and loungers
With bombs up their sleeves
Cut-throats and thieves
They are not
Welcome here
We should make them
Go back to where they came from
They cannot
Share our food
Share our homes
Share our countries
Instead let us
Build a wall to keep them out
It is not okay to say
These are people just like us
A place should only belong to those who are born there
Do not be so stupid to think that
The world can be looked at another way

(*now read from bottom to top*)

Brian Bilston (20th/21st century)

Love in the Time of Cauliflower

Please marrow me, my beloved sweetpea,
so that we may beetroot to our hearts.
Lettuce have the courgette of our convictions
and our love elevated to Great Artichoke.

Don't leek me feeling this way, my dear,
such lofty asparagus can't be ignored.
I am a prisoner, trapped in your celery;
Don't make me go back to the drawing broad beans.

We all carry emotional cabbage:
love is chard and not inconsequential,
but may our passion be uncucumbered
so that we reach our true potato.

Oh, how your onions make my head spinach,
reduce me to mushrooms, broccoli, defenceless.
Only you can salsify my desire,
and I, in turnip, will radish you senseless.

love poem, inadvertently written with auto-carrot switched on

Brain Bilston (20th/21st century)

Politicians

Hear hear, ra ra ra
Jolly jolly, fa fa fa
Yes yes, no no,
First speaker – you may go

Bla bla bla, I'm such a toff
Ya ya, cough cough
Fa fa fa, I'm very rich
Jolly jolly, twitch twitch

Bla bla bla 'A better year'
Knock knock 'hear hear'
Fa fa fa 'turn things around'
Clap clap. Sit down

Clap clap. Next one on
Bla bla. He's wrong
Fa fa fa pause pause
'I'm right'. Big applause

Bla bla I've got 6 cars
Jolly jolly fa fa
Pause pause. Wait wait
Cough cough. Kids are great

Bla bla big applause
Fa fa 'better laws'
'Hear hear' bench taps
Sit down. Clap clap

Next one up 'I don't agree'
Ra ra 'Vote for me'
Bla bla 'cos I can'
bang my fists down like a man

Ya ya well I can lean
Ra ra to make it seem
like what I say is really good
Clap clap. Tap the wood

I wave my hand up in the air
to make it look like you should care
or point my finger round instead
to give some worth to what I've said

Bla bla 'I see I see'
Good Lord! In fact you're just like me
You're dull, you're grey, you're almost dead
You never did those things you said

You 'want us equal, want fair rules'
and send your kids to public schools
you moan about 'the country's state'
books for schools, the time you wait

in hospitals, the lack of care
although *you* don't get treated there
you promise them you have a plan
but you've stretched the budget all you can

'There's no more money left' you say
'Except all that, but that's my pay'
'Jolly show, I'm just like you
– are you a politician too?'

Hollie McNish (21st century)

The Instructions

1. How to spot THE INSTRUCTIONS

THE INSTRUCTIONS come in all shapes and sizes. They are often found in and around:

- *Tall buildings with statues of lions outside*
- *Faces with an angry expression*
- *Faces with a smile seen only in the mouth but (crucially) not in the eyes*

2. The other instructions

There are plenty of *other* sorts of instructions, which can of course be useful.

For example:

- *Try not to insert any part of your body into this pond: it contains an irritated crocodile*
- *For best results, keep both eyes open while landing this lopsided helicopter*
- *Do not under any circumstances eat the angry man's sandwich*

3. What THE INSTRUCTIONS want

You see, THE INSTRUCTIONS aren't here to help you. They want to help someone or something else.
THE INSTRUCTIONS say things like:

- *No one's ever done THAT before: it CAN'T be a good idea.*
- *Please do the SAME thing as all those OTHER people over THERE*
- *Hear that person talking in the PARTICULARLY loud voice? They must DEFINITELY be RIGHT.*

4. If you follow THE INSTRUCTIONS

If you follow THE INSTRUCTIONS it is unlikely
anyone will ever be very cross with you.
If you follow THE INSTRUCTIONS you are
guaranteed to feel neat and tidy (but also a little
short of breath).

5. If you do not follow THE INSTRUCTIONS

You will likely face some tricky moments. Apologies for this.
However, there is also a good chance that something

> strangeexcitingremarkableunexpectedslightly-
> frighteningbutbrightlycoloured

will happen.

6. The choice

is yours.

Kate Wakeling (20th/21st century)

the parents anniversary

that on the last day of july
my father would tell the story
of how they had met
so young in photos i once saw
of an eighties blurred with rain
and home haircuts
how easily she had made
her impression and left it there
      that years later he would
follow her to pulsing cities
and countries now closed
to the rest of the world
      that they would marry
dress each other in light
a day so hot that sand
could boil to glass
she, a striped cat who purrs
he, a tamed bear.
      that they could repeat these words
a little different year by year
but by the same stellate night
that he could sleep in
the fourth chamber of her heart
and stay there and stay there

Lucy Thynne (21st century)